The ART of the BAR

The ART of the BAR

COCKTAILS INSPIRED BY THE CLASSICS

BY THE BARTENDERS OF ABSINTHE BRASSERIE & BAR

 JEFF HOLLINGER & ROB SCHWARTZ

FOREWORD BY GEORGEANNE BRENNAN

PHOTOGRAPHS BY FRANKIE FRANKENY

CHRONICLE BOOKS

SAN FRANCISCO

LIBRARY OF CONGRESS CATALOGING-IN-PUBLICATION DATA AVAILABLE.

ISBN-10: 0-8118-5498-1
ISBN-13: 978-0-8118-5498-6

MANUFACTURED IN CHINA.

PRODUCED BY PIPER KELLER
FOOD STYLING BY ROBIN VALERIK AND ALISON RICHMAN
DESIGNED BY JULIA FLAGG

The photographer wishes to thank BILL RUSSELL-SHAPIRO, GEORGEANNE BRENNAN, JEFF HOLLINGER and ROB SCHWARTZ, JULIA FLAGG, LESLIE JONATH, DESIRAE BEBERNISS, HA HUYNH, JOANN FRANKENY, and CAMI HAECKER.

DISTRIBUTED IN CANADA BY RAINCOAST BOOKS
9050 Shaughnessy Street
Vancouver, British Columbia V6P 6E5

10 9 8 7 6 5 4 3 2

CHRONICLE BOOKS LLC
85 Second Street
San Francisco, California 94105

www.chroniclebooks.com

ACKNOWLEDGMENTS

We would like to thank our wives and families for their love and support; and Billy and Alice Russell Shapiro; Ross Browne; Marcovaldo Dionosis for starting everything behind Absinthe's bar; Frankie Frankeny; Julia Flagg; Georgeanne Brennan; Chronicle Books; all of the bartenders who've stepped behind the bar at Absinthe, as well as the entire staff at the restaurant; our guests and regulars over the years who have inspired, acted as tasting panels, and become part of the family, spending days and nights bellied up to the bar as we developed many of the cocktails in this book; every bartender past and present who's had the willingness to expand and inspire the trade; and special thanks to Jonny Raglin for manning the helm, picking up where we left off with his creativity and consistent drive to expand Absinthe's cocktail program.

CONTENTS

COCKTAIL MENU

21 hayes / 103
pimm's no. 1, cucumber, plymouth gin, lemon juice

31 flavors / 123
gin, pimm's no. 1, velvet falernum, peach and orange bitters, grapefruit, cranberry, and orange juice, cointreau

84 and hazy / 89
apricot, rum, lime juice, mulberry syrup, cointreau

the 100 percent cocktail / 83
swedish punch, orange and lemon juice

agave rose / 80
tequila, cherry brandy, lime juice, velvet falernum

americano / 30
campari, sweet vermouth, soda water

astoria / 51
gin, dry vermouth, orange bitters

aviation / 44
gin, maraschino liqueur, lemon juice

back-porch lemonade / 121
ginger syrup, lemon and cranberry juice, citron vodka, ginger ale

battle of new orleans / 43
bourbon, herbsaint, peychaud's bitters, orange bitters, anisette

black bomber / 132
light gin, anisette, espresso

the blackout / 129
151 proof rum, amaretto, grand marnier, tea, white crème de cacao, cream

blood and sand / 101
scotch, cherry brandy, sweet vermouth, orange juice

bloody mary / 137
vodka, tomato juice, dijon, horseradish, spices

bobby burns / 95
scotch, bénédictine, sweet vermouth

bob-tailed nag / 125
michter's single-barrel straight rye whiskey, cocchi barolo chinato, mint bitters

bored stiff / 134
tawny port, amaretto, white crème de cacao, orange bitters

brazil 66 / 57
cachaça, lime, cointreau, orange juice

bronx bomber / 24
plymouth gin, sweet and dry vermouth, orange and lemon juice

buster brown / 83
bourbon, lemon juice, orange bitters

caipirinha / 83
cachaça, lime

candied apple / 130
calvados, caramel syrup, berentzen apfel korn liqueur

castaway / 80
montecristo 12-year-old rum, mango, agave syrup, lime juice

character / 108
glenmorangie scotch, cocchi aperitivo americano, bitters

choke artist / 97
cynar, gran centenario anejo tequila, fino sherry, orange bitters

cosmopolitan / 25
citrus vodka, triple sec, cranberry and lime juice

daedalus / 123
irish whiskey, ginger syrup, orange bitters

dapper apple / 89
citadelle apple vodka, triple sec, lime juice

death in the afternoon / 139
pastis, champagne

devil's own / 135
orange brandy, reposado tequila, hot chocolate, frangelico, sweetened heavy cream

devil's pearl / 84
absente, anisette, angostura bitters

dr. schwartz's cherry-vanilla bitters / 32
rye, vanilla, cherry bark, cardamom, anise, ginger, quassia

dunlop / 97
rum, sherry, orange bitters

el presidente / 98
ron pampero aniversario rum, sweet vermouth, peychaud's bitters

elixir no. 1 / 84
averna, sweet vermouth, campari, velvet falernum, orange bitters

elixir no. 2 / 134
gin, brandy, crème de menthe, maraschino liqueur

fig thyme / 123
fig, pisco, cointreau, thyme syrup, lime juice

french 75 / 36
gin, champagne, lemon juice, cherries

galapagos / 112
kaffir lime leaf, pepper syrup, pisco, lime and grapefruit juice, brandied cherries

ginger rogers / 41
gin, mint, lime, ginger ale

grand slam / 98
swedish punch, dry and sweet vermouth

havana / 42
gosling's rum, cointreau, orange and lime juice

hot toddy / 135
brandy, cloves, cinnamon, star anise, honey, lemon

intosato noce / 134
plymouth gin, oloroso sherry, cynar, orange bitters

jitney jumble / 57
basil hayden bourbon, iced tea, kirsch, crème de cacao

jonny's apple seed / 110
calvados, apple, lemon juice

key lime pie / 131
key limes, charbay key lime vodka, sylk cream liqueur, liquor 43

la floridita daiquiri / 101
rum, lime juice, maraschino liqueur, grapefruit juice

last call / 134
calvados, tuaca, orange bitters

lavender sidecar / 120
brandy, lavender honey syrup, lemon juice, orange bitters, cointreau

le démon vert / 67
broker's gin, absente, velvet falernum, lime juice

lemon meringue / 130
hangar 1 buddha's hand citron vodka, lemon juice, sylk cream liqueur

the little easy / 107
single malt scotch, orange bitters, averna, herbsaint

margarita / 26
silver tequila, cointreau, lime juice

martinez / 19
plymouth gin, dolin dry vermouth, orange bitters, maraschino liqueur

martini / 19
gin, dry vermouth

mint julep / 51
bourbon, mint

mississippi mule / 98
gin, crème de cassis, lemon juice

monte carlo / 84
rye, bénédictine, peychaud's bitters

mujer verde / 73
hendrick's gin, lime juice, yellow and green chartreuse

mulberry street sling / 124
gin, mulberry syrup, lemon juice

negroni / 31
junipero gin, campari, punt e mes

nevada / 57
rum, grapefruit and lime juice, angostura bitters

new pal / 92
rye, campari, sweet vermouth, peychaud's bitters, pastis

nickel rose / 83
campari, aquavit, peach bitters, velvet falernum, lime and grapefruit juice

oaxacan / 130
talapa mescal, pimm's no. 1, peychaud's bitters

old-fashioned / 20
bourbon, orange, brandied cherries, sugar, angostura bitters

old pal / 92
canadian whisky, campari, dry vermouth

opera / 23
gin, red dubonnet, maraschino liqueur, orange bitters

paddle boat / 45
bourbon, orange juice, mathilde framboise, crème de cacao

peaches & herb / 71
fresh peach, sage, brandy, lemon juice, cointreau

pearanha / 124
spiced rum, clear creek pear brandy, ginger, orange and lime juice

pergroni / 123
campari, pernod, sweet vermouth, orange bitters

pisco sour / 79
pisco, egg white, lime, angostura bitters

plantation / 78
plymouth gin, basil leaves, cointreau, lime and grapefruit juice

quarterdeck / 98
rum, sherry, lime juice, angostura bitters

ramos gin fizz / 81
gin, egg white, cream, lime, orange-flower water

rosebud / 110
silver tequila, rosewater, sweet vermouth, campari

rum crusta / 75
charbay vanilla rum, cointreau, maraschino liqueur, lemon juice

salty poodle / 51
tequila, lime and grapefruit juice, fee brothers falernum, cointreau

sangre de fresa / 117
strawberries, basil leaves, balsamic syrup, cachaça, cointreau, lime juice

sazerac / 16
rye, peychaud's bitters, herbsaint

sensation / 84
gin, mint, lime, maraschino liqueur

sherry twist cocktail no. 1 / 96
sherry, brandy, dry vermouth, cointreau, cinnamon, lemon juice

singapore sling / 33
gin, benedictine, cherry brandy, pineapple and lime juice, grenadine, angostura bitters

sleepyhead / 67
brandy, ginger ale, mint, lemon

sour cherry blossom / 110
cognac, sour cherry syrup, lemon juice

spanish coffee / 130
151 proof rum, cinnamon, hot coffee, kahlúa, sweetened cream

stockholm / 51
charbay meyer lemon vodka, lemon juice, chilled champagne

tequila gimlet de grenada / 110
el tesoro platinum tequila, pomegranate liqueur, lime juice

tim tam / 115
montecristo 12-year-old rum, citronage, tamarind syrup, agave syrup, black tea

tomato kiss / 111
silver tequila, sweet 100 tomatoes, cilantro leaves, lime juice, cointreau

trilby no. 2 / 97
scotch, marie brizard parfait amour, absente, vermouth, orange bitters

"uptown" manhattan / 22
maker's mark bourbon, sweet vermouth, angostura bitters

velvet orange / 57
hangar 1 mandarin blossom vodka, orange brandy, orange and lime juice, velvet falernum

venetian / 97
gin, campari, dry vermouth, amaretto

FOREWORD

BY GEORGEANNE BRENNAN

JEFF HOLLINGER AND ROB SCHWARTZ, ACCOMPLISHED MIXOLOGISTS OF TODAY'S COCKTAIL GENERATION, bring us their passionate take on the art of the bar, an art that combines history, creativity, intuition, and conviviality. Going with them through the pages of *The Art of the Bar* is like being at Absinthe's bar, where they rule supreme, surrounded by a rollicking before- or after-theater crowd delightedly drinking the concoctions, classic and creative, that Jeff and Rob pass across the copper. But the book also reveals the quieter moments at Absinthe, where late afternoons and early evenings find lovers and friends in close conversations over drinks and colleagues at after-office-hours cocktail meetings. Rob and Jeff are there for the late morning and lunchtime crowd too, creating, passing out recipes, always sharing their passion and expertise for the bar. Join them at Absinthe and discover the past, present, and future of the art of the bar.

Cocktails have long been considered soignée and sophisticated, perhaps because of their association with the glamorous capitals of the world or with the forbidden but brief period of the speakeasies during Prohibition in the United States. They are deeply embedded in our culture, part of the romance of our history, and their names are associated with cities, places, and people, including fictional ones. The MINT JULEP conjures up the Kentucky Derby, MANHATTAN the heart of New York City, MARGARITAS our love affair with South of the Border, and the MARTINI has become indelibly associated with James Bond.

As HOLLINGER and SCHWARTZ take us through the history of the classic cocktails, we learn such tidbits as a Tom Collins was originally concocted to cover the raw taste of the gin of the day, and that the SAZERAC, one of Absinthe's most popular drinks and considered the first cocktail, was made originally with Cognac, later with rye whiskey, when the phylloxera louse devastated the vineyards in France and sharply reduced the production of Cognac. The stories behind the OLD-FASHIONED, COSMOPOLITAN, MANHATTAN, and the MARGARITA are related in witty detail as our guides behind the bar reveal not only the past and present versions of these drinks but the principles upon which they are based, and how contemporary bartenders like them have developed their own creations as well as variations on the classics, such as Absinthe's hallmark "UPTOWN" MANHATTAN.

HOLLINGER and SCHWARTZ take us to the other side of the bar, showing us how they work. Behind the polished counter we learn to distinguish among possets, slings and shrubs, Collins and cobblers, chillers, fizzes, and highballs. With the able assistance of HOLLINGER and SCHWARTZ, muddlers, pouring spouts, cocktail shakers, and Hawthorne Strainers become our familiars, and we become well-versed in the four basic types of ice and when to use which. Our mentors open the bottles that line Absinthe's bar wall, explaining how all the spirits, from absinthe to whiskey, are made and the nuances within each. Tequila, for example, is a controlled denomination of origin, regulated by the Mexican government. Five of the Mexican states are allowed to make it and must use the blue agave plant. Some tequilas are made with 100 percent blue agave, others with blue agave and sugars. Some are aged, others, like Silver Tequila, are not.

Cocktails are complex. To make them requires not only knowledge of the spirits, the recipes, skillful pouring, measuring, whether to shake or stir, but a sound knowledge of what makes a good drink. HOLLINGER and SCHWARTZ rely on fresh ingredients and make their basics from scratch whenever feasible. We are encouraged to use fresh fruit and herbs in season, when they are at their peak of flavor. They teach us to make our own syrups, bitters, and blends from scratch, and how to set up a home bar. Our lessons behind the bar are sprinkled with anecdotes, tips for home mixologists, and inspiration to make our own concoctions.

I can't think of a more pleasant, comprehensive, and entertaining way to enter into the magical world behind the bar than this book, sharing the experiences of experts while developing my own sure hand at making classic cocktails and inventing new ones. I'll sit down with HOLLINGER and SCHWARTZ anytime, my elbows on the bar at Absinthe, or their book in my hand, sipping a concoction while I watch them deftly pouring and polishing, talking and listening.

THE SPIRITS OF
ABSINTHE

TO THE UNINITIATED,

BARTENDING MAY SEEM LIKE

A MYSTERIOUS TRADE.

WE MIX OUR POTIONS

BY COMBINING SPIRITS, JUICES, AND SYRUPS

WITH DASHES OF THIS

AND

DROPS OF THAT.

1

THE BAR HERE AT ABSINTHE IS AN ONGOING WORK-IN-PROGRESS. IT IS built on tradition, honor, and the long history of the classic cocktail. Nestled among the boutique shops of San Francisco's Hayes Valley, Absinthe Brasserie & Bar has long been known as the place to go for a creative cocktail and a romantic dinner.

From behind the bar, as we're conceiving cocktails and washing glassware, some guests pour out the intimacies of their lives before we even learn their names. The best of us can lend a sympathetic ear to one customer while quickly and skillfully producing an endless assortment of cocktails for everyone else. The next time we see the guest who needed to talk, he may be a little embarrassed about his earlier confessions, but if we pour his favorite poison before he asks and hand it to him with a smile, we'll see him again and again. This is an element of the art of the bar—creating a welcoming, convivial atmosphere. Another is the allure of the perfect elixir, which we strive for on a daily basis.

COCKTAIL EXPLORERS

FROM THE FIRST TIME WE EACH PICKED UP A SHAKER behind the bar, we loved the vibe. We also welcomed the management's encouragement to explore age-old cocktails and adapt classic recipes for today's palate. Over the years we've built up a reputation for creating some of the best examples of classic and classically inspired cocktails in San Francisco.

Our drinks contain at least a dash of the late-eighteenth and early-nineteenth centuries, when some of America's most treasured cocktails were first created. Our knowledge of the past connects us with our bartending forefathers—their creations and traditions. When we stir up a **MARTINEZ,** for example, we are creating what many consider to be the father of the quintessential cocktail, the **MARTINI.**

Our reverence for the classics doesn't dampen our enthusiasm for experimenting, however. Hardly a night goes by behind the bar when someone isn't testing or tinkering with something new. We are the mad scientists with bottles and shakers strewn before us, stirring potion after potion until we find the perfect combination to send a customer's tastebuds on a euphoric journey. Like good chefs, we try new ingredients, presentations, and various combinations of liquors in order to create the next great cocktail. When we seek out "new" recipes in old cocktail books, pursue new combinations of fresh and local ingredients, or dabble with new liquors, we are taking an active role in the evolution of the cocktail. As we see it, we are cocktail explorers, fortune-hunting our way through history and pouring our discoveries for future imbibers.

Typically, our new cocktails are born in early evening as guests share stories with friends, laughing and clinking glasses, creating a lyrical backdrop to the music of our shakers. A weary suit with his tie pulled loose at his neck, or a dolled-up twenty-something waiting for her friends to arrive, will sit down at the bar. Pulling a crinkled recipe from a pocket, he or she will shyly slide it across the copper bar and ask if we can make that cocktail. If the recipe is for a drink that we have never sipped before, the guest immediately becomes a source of inspiration and an expert taster. All suggestions are received with respect and open ears.

Once we all taste the drink, the discussion begins. Adjustments are made, sometimes at the direction of the guest, and sometimes as a result of our intuition. As the evening creeps toward nighttime, the redesigned drink goes through any number of changes. The way we look at it, half of the fun and all of the learning

in mixing cocktails lies in tasting the successes and the failures, and then trying again.

Regulars will often sit down at the bar and ask us for a glass of whatever is being tested that evening. This sharing of knowledge and time reflects the true spirit of Absinthe and explains why the atmosphere here is always so inviting. We even print cocktail recipes directly from our register's printer and offer them to guests who want them for their next shindig or to add to their collection of favorites. Sometimes we present a recipe as a surprise. Once the guest realizes it's not a check, we are usually greeted with a sprightly smile and heartfelt thanks!

Some may think it strange that we're willing to give out recipes, but in doing so we help people appreciate some of Absinthe's core cocktail philosophies: We're passionate about understanding the ingredients we use and make sure they are fresh. We strive for balance, and are always willing to experiment.

SAZERAC

1 sugar cube
5 dashes Peychaud's bitters
2 ounces rye
Herbsaint
Lemon twist for garnish

———————— MAKES 1 DRINK ————————

Fill an old-fashioned glass or cocktail glass with ice and top with water. In a second old-fashioned glass, combine the sugar and the bitters, and muddle to dissolve the sugar. Add the rye and gently stir to combine the flavors. Discard the ice and water from the first glass and coat it with the Herbsaint, draining the excess. Strain the rye mixture into this glass. Rub the rim with the lemon peel. If you're a purist, discard the peel as they do in New Orleans. If not, drop it into the drink.

ADAPTED FROM *FAMOUS NEW ORLEANS DRINKS AND HOW TO MIX 'EM* (1937), BY STANLEY CLISBY ARTHUR.

TALES OF COCKTAILS PAST

WHEN AMERICANS BEGAN DRINKING COCKTAILS in the late 1800s, they were nothing more than a style of drink, much like a punch, fizz, or cobbler. The defining elements of the cocktail were a base spirit, sugar, water, and bitters. At first it seemed an odd curiosity because many of its advocates treated it like morning drink, something that you imbibed as the rooster crowed its welcome to a new day. Imagine pushing aside your morning bowl of cereal and replacing it with a stomach-warming whiskey cocktail! Back then, however, the cocktail was generally consumed by hustling, hard-drinking men who probably needed a nip of the "hair of the dog" to shake off the previous night's follies. It seems we've come a long way from those days, considering the status and sophistication the cocktail now enjoys and the range that goes well beyond a Vodka Tonic or Perfect Manhattan.

We consider the **SAZERAC** the first truly important cocktail, making its appearance in New Orleans about 1860. It was made with Cognac, since that was the most readily available spirit of the time, and eventually included a dash of absinthe, which explains our own fondness for this drink. Within a few short years, however, Cognac fell out of favor and rye became the primary spirit in the cocktail. This was mainly due to a vine-eating parasite known as phylloxera, which greatly reduced Cognac production in France and caused prices to soar. Never to be denied their drink, bartenders looked toward a growing production of rye here in the States and realized that it would make an excellent substitute in a cocktail that by 1900 was almost a classic.

The word "cocktail" itself stems from dubious beginnings. There are nearly as many stories about its origin as there are cocktails in the world. Sazerac-lovers claim that the word drives from the French *coquetier,* the eggcup with a wide base that was turned upside down to serve their favorite drink. We like to tell the story of Betsy Flanagan, a tavern-keeper during the American Revolution who garnished her drinks with a rooster's tail feather. The soldiers were so enamored of her drinks that they would toast her with the chant **"Vive le coqtail!"** Perhaps the word comes from a combination of the Colonial word "cock," a tap for pouring spirits, and "tailings," the last offerings from the barrel. When someone needed a cheap drink, the *tailings* would be pulled from each cock and mixed together; these offerings were dubbed "cocktails."

The **MARTINI,** a venerable cocktail icon, is arguably one of the easiest drinks to make. Take a large dose of gin, a splash of vermouth, stir until cold, and strain into a chilled cocktail glass. Add an olive or a twist and you've got a **MARTINI**. It should be that simple, but more arguments have made their way across the bar, and more has been written about how to mix the perfect Martini than about any other cocktail in the world. James Bond's famous opinion was to insist that you use vodka and shake it. The combination of simplicity and strong personal preferences is obviously the right recipe for a cocktail controversy!

The exact story of where the Martini was born will be forever debated, but we think it was most likely a variation of the Martinez cocktail, developed by the legendary turn-of-the-century bartender Jerry Thomas in San Francisco's Occidental Hotel sometime in the late 1800s. His drink was made with a gin, sweetened to hide impurities, known as Old Tom; sweet vermouth; orange bitters; and a splash of maraschino liqueur. The gin-to-vermouth ratio was about two-to-one, and sometimes it went as low as one-to-one.

Pour this version for self-respecting martini connoisseurs now, and they would consider it to be sickeningly sweet. They need not worry, however, since it would be nearly impossible to recreate Thomas's exact recipe; Old Tom gin has virtually vanished from store shelves, and when it is found, it's viewed as more of an oddity than anything else. While the original recipe for the **MARTINEZ** is too sweet for most, we don't believe the Martinez should be poured down history's drain. On the contrary, we've developed a take on it that we feel is a perfect adaptation of a true classic. It is balanced, as a cocktail should be, and dry, as most of today's martini drinkers prefer them.

Time and tastes dictated the Martini's evolution toward the stripped-down, silver-streak drink we now see in bars and homes across America. During the late 1800s, Martinis were made with sweet vermouth, but by the first decade of the twentieth century, recipes for a Dry Martini, with dry vermouth, started to appear in cocktail books. Up until the 1940s, a Dry Martini was typically made with nearly two parts gin, one part vermouth, and a dash of orange bitters. By today's standards, a Martini mixed in this style is anything but dry. It wasn't until the Cold War era of the 1950s that the vermouth was reduced to a nearly molecular amount. During that same period there was another big change in the evolution of the Martini: Vodka began replacing gin. By the 1970s, the Vodka Martini was a standard drink.

Today, the Martini has reached such status that the classic V-shaped cocktail glass used for serving the drink is a universally recognized symbol; it has even adopted the name "martini glass." More recently, the Martini has

MARTINEZ

2 ounces Plymouth gin

1 ounce Dolin dry vermouth

Splash of maraschino liqueur

Dash of orange bitters

Lemon twist for garnish

Olive for garnish

—————— MAKES 1 DRINK ——————

Combine all the liquid ingredients in an ice-filled cocktail shaker. Stir gently for 20 to 30 seconds, until cold, and then strain into a chilled cocktail glass. Garnish with the lemon twist and olive.

MARTINI

2 ounces gin

¼ ounce dry vermouth

Olive or lemon twist for garnish

—————— MAKES 1 DRINK ——————

Combine the gin and vermouth in an ice-filled cocktail shaker. Stir gently for 20 to 30 seconds, until cold, and strain into a chilled cocktail glass. Garnish with the olive or lemon twist.

OLD-FASHIONED

1 sugar cube
1 orange slice
2 dashes Angostura bitters
1 to 2 brandied cherries (optional, PAGE 76)
1½ ounces bourbon

——————— MAKES 1 DRINK ———————

In an old-fashioned glass, muddle the sugar cube with the orange slice, bitters, and cherries, if using. Add ice, top with the bourbon, and stir to mix.

experienced a linguistic change similar to that of the cocktail. Nowadays, just about anything served in a martini glass is dubbed a Martini. Die-hard devotees surely cringe at the idea of calling vanilla vodka mixed with Midori and a mélange of fruit juices a melon Martini. While we shy away from making drinks of this style, we think the tendency to call them "martinis" simply reflects the influence of the most revered of all cocktails.

The **OLD-FASHIONED** is another of our favorite classics. Legend has it that this cocktail was first made at the Pendennis Club in Louisville, Kentucky, during the late 1800s, in honor of a well-known whiskey proprietor, Colonel James E. Pepper. The bartender dissolved a bit of sugar with a few spoonfuls of water, added a dash of Angostura bitters, a jigger of whiskey, and a lump of ice. Finally, he stirred in a lemon peel. While Colonel Pepper was surely honored by the presentation of this cocktail, it was probably not the first time it had been made.

The drink presented to the Colonel was really nothing more than a Whiskey Cocktail, made in the old-fashioned style. Long before Colonel Pepper sipped on his Old-Fashioned, a "cocktail" was a drink that comprised any spirit, plus sugar, water, and bitters. It took several years before the word "cocktail" became a generic term for any number of drinks. The Old-Fashioned Whiskey Cocktail was nothing more than a version of a cocktail—in the original sense of the word—made with whiskey. So by the time it was "invented" at the Pendennis Club, the Old-Fashioned was nearly one hundred years old! Whether the bartender who presented Colonel Pepper with the Old-Fashioned was aware this was actually an age-old drink remains one of the great debates surrounding it.

With nearly two centuries' worth of history under the Old-Fashioned's glass, it is no surprise the drink has seen its share of variations and debatable ingredients. The standard versions usually involve muddling a bitters-soaked sugar cube with an orange slice and a cherry. The mash is then topped with ice and a shot of bourbon is stirred in. Recipes have ranged from these straightforward incarnations to concoctions made with pineapple sticks, orange curaçao, and absinthe. As far as we are concerned, an Old-Fashioned can be made as simply or as elaborately as you like. If you'd like peach bitters and a slice of peach muddled in yours, we're happy to oblige. We all have our preferences. When mixing one for ourselves, for example, we tend to use rye in place of bourbon, and we like the added sweetness from the muddled orange. We'll include brandied cherries when we have them on hand, but we never dilute our Old-Fashioneds with water.

"UPTOWN" MANHATTAN

2 ounces bourbon, preferably Maker's Mark

1 ounce Carpano Antica sweet vermouth

Dash of Angostura bitters

Dash of orange bitters

3 brandied cherries (PAGE 76) for garnish

Orange twist for garnish

——— MAKES 1 DRINK ———

Combine all the liquid ingredients in an ice-filled cocktail shaker. Stir gently for 20 to 30 seconds, until cold, and then strain into a chilled cocktail glass. Garnish with the cherries and orange twist.

The **MANHATTAN** is a sublime cocktail and, amazingly, its recipe has remained almost unchanged over the past century. Called the father of the Martinez and the grandfather of the Martini, the Manhattan was originally a mixture of rye, sweet vermouth, and bitters. Today a bourbon like Jim Beam or Maker's Mark usually replaces the rye. This change in spirits probably occurred after Prohibition, when rye was less readily available. We know bartenders who will argue this point, but we believe either spirit is acceptable in a Manhattan; rye will provide a spicier, more robust cocktail, while bourbon yields a sweeter, mellower cocktail.

Perhaps the biggest mistake we see people make when mixing Manhattans is excluding the bitters. We don't know whether a home bartender leaves it out because he doesn't understand the cocktail or because he doesn't have bitters in his repertoire, but either way the omission is a shame. Without bitters, the Manhattan lacks the characteristically herbaceous flavor that makes it one of the most popular cocktails mixed today. And most important, a properly made Manhattan is the basis of many cocktails, including some of Absinthe's signature concoctions.

No one knows exactly when the Manhattan was invented, but it's thought to have first appeared sometime in the mid- to late-1800s, around the time that Italian, or sweet, vermouth was gaining popularity with New York's bartending community. According to many accounts, the drink was created in 1874 at a party hosted by Winston Churchill's mother at the Manhattan Club to celebrate Samuel Tilden's victory in New York's gubernatorial election.

This story has all the glitz, glamor, and celebratory hoopla that are appropriate for the birth of a great cocktail, but it is probably not true. Tilden did win the governor's election, there was a party thrown in his honor hosted by Churchill's mother, and Manhattans were even poured at the party, but probably not for the first time. According to cocktail historians, a bartender named Black who operated a saloon on Broadway in the mid-1800s was mixing Manhattans years before Tilden's party. It's possible that both of these stories are true, and that the Manhattan originated in more than one place during the same period. Or maybe Tilden's party just made it popular. It is common, though, when bartenders are working with similar ingredients, for nearly identical cocktails to develop in a number of places, independently of one another. After all, sweet vermouth was a newcomer behind the bar, and surely intuitive bartenders were experimenting with it in countless cocktails, just as we do today.

OPERA

1½ ounces gin
½ ounce red Dubonnet
¼ ounce maraschino liqueur
Dash of orange bitters
Orange twist for garnish

——— MAKES 1 DRINK ———

In an ice-filled cocktail shaker, combine
all the liquid ingredients. Stir for 20 to 30
seconds, until cold, and then strain into a
chilled champagne flute. Garnish with the
orange twist.

OUR RECIPE IS FROM *THE OFFICIAL MIXER'S MANUAL* (PATRICK
GAVIN DUFFY, 1934).

BRONX BOMBER

1½ ounces Plymouth gin

¼ ounce Italian sweet vermouth

¼ ounce French dry vermouth

½ ounce fresh orange juice

¼ ounce fresh lemon juice

¼ ounce Simple Syrup (PAGE 116)

Orange twist for garnish

—————— MAKES 1 DRINK ——————

Combine all the liquid ingredients in an ice-filled cocktail shaker. Shake until cold, and then strain into a chilled cocktail glass. Garnish with the orange twist.

A VARIATION OF THE BRONX COCKTAIL FROM *OLD WALDORF-ASTORIA BAR BOOK* BY ALBERT STEVENS CROCKETT, 1935.

The **BRONX**, another vintage cocktail, is resurfacing eighty years after its heyday during Prohibition. This gin-based mixture with sweet and dry vermouth and a healthy dose of orange juice was one of the most heavily consumed cocktails during the thirteen years of America's "noble experiment." And for good reason. Gin reigned supreme during Prohibition since it was easy and inexpensive to make, and it could be consumed almost immediately upon its release from the still. At the time, nearly every establishment serving illegal hooch also had orange juice and some form of vermouth, so the Bronx was a no-brainer of a cocktail.

Almost immediately upon Prohibition's repeal, however, the Bronx was shunned by the drinking world and dubbed one of the ten worst cocktails of the age. We can only assume that the Bronx received such harsh criticism because when the choices were once again limitless, critics wanted no part of the few drinks they were forced to consume time and again during America's dry spell. Although it will probably never gain the stature of drinks like the **MARTINI** or the **MANHATTAN**, the Bronx should be embraced as an important player in the history of the cocktail.

This drink is lighter and more quaffable than many of the classics, and it was probably a welcome refresher on a hot New York afternoon, such as the one on which it was created. Cocktail historians are, amazingly, in almost universal agreement that Johnny Solon, a bartender at the old Waldorf-Astoria in the late 1890s, shook up the drink after being challenged by a lunch customer to create something new. Having just finished mixing a Duplex, which comprised equal parts of French and Italian vermouths and a twist of orange peel, Solon was obviously tinkering with variations when he came up with his new drink. To create the Bronx—so named because of his visit to the Bronx Zoo a few days earlier—he reduced the amount of vermouth and added gin and a healthy dose of orange juice.

Today you're likely to find a bartender mixing a more refined and less juicy version with better gin. In our own **BRONX BOMBER** we've added simple syrup and lemon juice to the mix and reduced the amount of orange juice in order to unify all the ingredients in the cocktail and highlight the qualities of some of our specialty gins. For a lighter cocktail, leave out the simple syrup and lemon and up the OJ levels, as Solon did for his drink.

The **COSMOPOLITAN** has probably been America's most universally known and ordered cocktail of the past decade. While the mixture of vodka, Cointreau, fresh juice, and a splash of cranberry juice may lack a Manhattan's complexity, it is consistently refreshing with its light citrus overtones.

Thought to have first appeared on the cocktail scene sometime around the mid-1980s, the "Cosmo" could easily be called the newest classic cocktail. What does it take for a cocktail to be considered a classic? Ultimately, time. But in our opinion, there are at least a few criteria that can help a drink reach classic status. First, the cocktail should be born of questionable origins. Look at drinks like the **MARTINI, THE OLD-FASHIONED,** and the **MANHATTAN**—none of these cocktails has a definitive birthplace. Second, the potential classic should have nearly universal recognition. Place a cocktail glass on the bar, for example, and most people will automatically think of the Martini. The Old-Fashioned even has a glass named after it. Third, the classic cocktail must instigate never-ending conversations between cocktail geeks at bars, home cocktail parties, and online forums about how to construct the drink to perfection.

The Cosmopolitan achieved iconic status during the 1990s and early 2000s, thanks in part to the drink's constant appearance on hipster television shows like *Sex and the City*. The story of when and where the first one was poured will likely be forever disputed. There are some who say that the cocktail was first introduced in San Francisco in the 1980s, but there is no hard evidence. According to another legend, the drink was first made at a steakhouse in Minneapolis in 1975, when a young bartender just entering the trade added a bit of cranberry juice to a Kamikaze and presented it to a guest, who exclaimed, "How cosmopolitan!" upon tasting it.

Probably the most universally accepted story about the invention of the Cosmo credits a New York bartender, Toby Cecchini, with the honor, although he is quick to deny it, perhaps out of modesty. He says that what he did was create a variation on another cocktail of the same name. Sometime around 1987, he and a fellow bartender were experimenting with a cocktail from San Francisco that was made with vodka, Rose's lime juice, and grenadine. This would have been a sticky-sweet, unbalanced concoction for sure. To improve the cocktail, they started with a newly released Absolut Citron vodka, substituted fresh lime for the sweetened, added Cointreau for balance, and splashed just enough cranberry juice to give the drink a cotton-candy hue. The drink was an instant success, and before long people were demanding them throughout the city. Cecchini's cocktail was so successful that the recipe is now synonymous with Cosmopolitans sipped in bars around the world.

When it comes to mixing cocktails at home, the Cosmo tends to be the drink that even the most inexperienced bartender knows how to construct. It's beautiful, simple to assemble, and calls for readily available ingredients.

COSMOPOLITAN

1½ ounces citrus vodka
1 ounce triple sec
½ ounce fresh lime juice
Splash of cranberry juice
Lemon twist for garnish

———— MAKES 1 DRINK ————

Combine the vodka, triple sec, lime and cranberry juice in an ice-filled cocktail shaker. Shake vigorously for 20 to 30 seconds, until cold, and strain into a chilled cocktail glass. Garnish with the lemon twist.

MARGARITA

1½ ounces silver tequila

1 ounce Cointreau

½ ounce fresh lime juice

Splash of Simple Syrup
(optional, PAGE 116)

———————— MAKES 1 DRINK ————————

Combine all the ingredients in an ice-filled cocktail shaker. Shake until cold, and then strain into a chilled salt-rimmed cocktail glass.

Today, the cocktail lists in most bars and restaurants have a Cosmo or a similar drink comprising some type of flavored vodka and juice mutation. The variations are endless. Whether we like it or not, the **COSMOPOLITAN** managed to sneak in through the back door of the classic cocktail party and it will stay until last call.

Considered one of the last great creations from the magical age of the cocktail (about 1890 to 1940), a properly made **MARGARITA** is the quintessential example of how simplicity can equal excellence. A mixture of three parts good-quality silver tequila, two parts Cointreau, and one part fresh lime juice, this drink also represents a style of cocktail known as a sour. A sour incorporates a base spirit, a sugar, the "sour" lemon or lime juice, and a bit of water, which is usually added by the melting ice, which dilutes the cocktail.

When made properly, the Margarita is a small drink that is shaken and served in a salt-rimmed cocktail glass, or on the rocks in a small bucket-style glass. Contrary to the examples set by too many restaurant chains, Margaritas should not be neon blue, served in pint glasses, or poured from slushy machines. They shouldn't contain artificially sweet mixes and liqueurs or an endless assortment of fruit, and they shouldn't be made in a blender, which has ruined far too many Margaritas.

No one is sure from where the Margarita originally hails, as is true of so many classic cocktails, but there is plenty of speculation. One interesting story has it that a socialite named Margarita Sames had a party in her Acapulco vacation home in 1948 and asked guests to step behind the bar and try their hand at new creations. The winner of the party, obviously, was the Margarita. Another story that we like even more revolves around a showgirl named Marjorie King, who was allergic to all alcohol except tequila. Sometime around 1938 or 1939 she visited the Rancho del Gloria Bar in Rosarita Beach, Mexico, and asked the bartender to create something with tequila. The resulting drink was named Margarita, the closest Spanish equivalent of "Marjorie."

Whatever its origins, the Margarita gained immense popularity in the 1970s, due in large part to rumors that tequila had a hallucinogenic effect on the drinker. By the time people realized there was no truth to the rumors, the Margarita was an established staple in nearly every bartender's repertoire. Today it's one of the first drinks budding home and professional bartenders learn. It makes a good foundation for other popular drinks, such as the **SIDECAR** and Kamikaze. The drink's popularity has never waned, and that's a good thing. We can think of no other cocktail we'd rather sip on a warm summer afternoon while tending the coals of a barbecue.

Prohibition
and the Art of the Cocktail

PEOPLE OFTEN ASSUME THAT THE **1920**s were the glory days of the cocktail—an era defined by the kicky Charleston; flappers with bobbed hair, short dresses, and risqué makeup; and a secret society of speakeasies filled to the gills with men and women eager to knock back a strong drink concocted by an all-knowing bartender. But these images, typically depicted in Hollywood movies, couldn't be further from the truth. In reality, by January 17, 1920, when the "noble experiment" of Prohibition was set in motion, the grand age of the cocktail had nearly reached its unceremonious demise.

The Eighteenth Amendment to the Constitution, which forbade the production, sale, import, and export of alcoholic beverages, was the result of a century-long reform movement. It was led by a number of pro-temperance groups fighting against what they viewed as the evil effects of drink. When the amendment took effect in 1920, it hit the nation like a shot of Booker's, and was as sobering as bar lights kicked up full blast at two in the morning, signaling the end of a good time.

Overnight, consumption of beverages containing anything more than 0.05 percent alcohol was officially illegal. At almost the same instant, drinking and bar culture slipped underground, forcing ordinary citizens to act like outlaws.

While we hope there will never be another attempt at Prohibition, the experiment did have some unintended yet interesting results. For one, it brought women into the world of the bar. Prior to that period, men, and men only, did their drinking in saloons. Many towns even had laws forbidding women from entering them. During Prohibition, however, club-owners were not as selective about their clientele, especially since it was now illegal for *anyone* to consume alcohol. At the time a growing feminist movement had been spawned, ironically enough, by groups such as the Women's Christian Temperance Union. With her short hair and hemlines revealing her powdered knees, a new breed of woman—the illustrious flapper—set out to redefine the atmosphere of America's watering holes. There were even women who owned their own clubs during the Prohibition era.

Prohibition also changed what people drank. Before the passage of the Eighteenth Amendment, most Americans consumed as much, if not more, beer and wine per year as they did spirits. When the amendment went into effect, spirits quickly became the drink of choice for those in need of a quick nip, because they were easier to produce, required less storage space, and were easier to transport. At first, whiskey—generally made from rye—was the spirit of choice, but because whiskey had to be aged for a number of years in wooden barrels before it was palatable, gin eventually surpassed whiskey's appeal. Gin was cheap and easy to produce, and it could be consumed almost immediately upon removal from the still or the bathtub, whatever the case may have been!

During Prohibition, Americans were not only consuming stronger alcoholic beverages but also drinking more of them. Before then, at least in the upscale bars of cities like New York and San Francisco, a cocktail was thought of in much the same way as food—it was something to be savored. By outlawing alcohol, the U.S. government transformed drinking into a criminal activity. Now the goal was to drink as much as you could in a short period of time, because the prospect of being caught was always lurking in the background. Binge drinking became standard, and the next day's disheveled recovery showed that you were a rebellious member of an underground elite.

Speakeasies quickly replaced the saloons of the nineteenth century. During the "dry" years of Prohibition they outnumbered the previously existing saloons by about two to one. These clubs were illegal, and you were advised to "speak easy" about a club's existence as well as the person who fed you the information about the joint. Some claim that the cocktail rose to new levels of popularity and creativity during the era of the speakeasy, with bartenders adding countless ingredients to base liquors in order to hide their poor flavor. More interesting, we think, were the "setups" that clubs provided during this era of clandestine drinking. The glasses, ice, and ginger ale or water were sold to patrons for a price. Then customers were free to add their own hooch from a flask they kept discreetly tucked away in a coat pocket or a purse. Club owners operating in this manner ingeniously avoided prosecution by authorities because all they were guilty of selling were setups, not booze.

In general, Prohibition proved to be detrimental to the art of the American bar. A few bartenders moved underground to work in speakeasies and some traveled to Europe to practice their trade legally, but most serious bartenders stopped bartending altogether. They thought that continuing to work in the trade would compromise the position they'd come to love. **Bartenders were suddenly viewed by the general public as promoters of illicit substances.** We think the best reason to leave bartending back then was that the product bartenders had grown accustomed to working with was no longer available.

In many ways, the cocktail was kept alive during Prohibition by the few bartenders who moved to Europe to work on foreign shores. Perhaps the most famous of this group was Harry Craddock, the bartender who wrote *The Savoy Cocktail Book,* a great tome of classic recipes that continues to inspire us. Harry reigned as head barman at the Savoy Hotel in London during the 1920s, and wrote *The Savoy Cocktail Book* in 1930.

Thankfully, by the middle of 1932 national sentiment toward Prohibition was finally changing. America was in the depths of the Great Depression. It was clear that trying to enforce Prohibition laws was futile and a waste of money. Furthermore, the government was missing a chance to tax liquor because it was being sold as bootleg booze. On December 5, 1933, the Eighteenth Amendment was ratified, effectively repealing Prohibition. It was once again legal to have a drink in America.

This dark period in history was intended to reduce crime, provide a cure for the social ills caused by a nation of tipplers, and improve the overall health of the country. Gangsters like Al Capone, speakeasy club owners, and resourceful bootleggers would quickly prove, however, that thirteen years of Prohibition was a truly a colossal failure on all counts.

BITTERS

DURING PROHIBITION, ONE COULD QUENCH THE desire for a drink legally with a shot of bitters. Essentially, these were highly alcoholic tinctures made from a combination of herbs and roots. While they greatly enhanced a cocktail, they were also thought to have medicinal value. Despite their alcoholic content, these concoctions were considered tonics and were said to improve the appetite. So one could imbibe without fear of breaking the law or offending a teetotaler.

Bitters were marketed as digestive aids. Europeans long believed in the healing qualities of these herbal concoctions. In fact, absinthe and Chartreuse were first developed in the eighteenth century as cure-all elixirs. In the nineteenth century it became common practice in England to add a touch of herbal bitters to gin so that it could be marketed as medicinal liquor and would not be taxable.

In the United States, there were countless styles of bitters available, ranging from stomach bitters, kidney bitters, and liver bitters to rye, bourbon, and whiskey bitters. Each type was believed to protect or cure the consumer of a different ailment; wildly misleading advertisements helped perpetuate these beliefs.

Are any of the medicinal claims tied to bitters true? Well, thanks to the Food and Drug Act of 1906, bitters can no longer be marketed as health remedies, but they are still useful. A dash or two of bitters added to a glass of soda water or ginger ale is a great way to settle an upset stomach. It's even said that Angostura bitters can help cure hiccups. Just coat a lemon wedge with sugar, douse it with Angostura, and bite down on the lemon. While we have yet to see this remedy work in person, we know countless people who swear by the process! Remember, however, that bitters are highly alcoholic, often as strong as 80 to 90 proof, so they should not be consumed as beverages; nor should they be used in nonalcoholic beverages.

When it came to mixing drinks around the turn of the century, bartenders understood the value of bitters. As we just noted, there were countless types, and bartending manuals often provided recipes for homemade bitters.

At Absinthe, we consider bitters one of the most important staples behind the bar. With their dry, bittersweet zing, they lend depth and complexity to many cocktails. A **MANHATTAN**, for example, simply would not be the same drink if it weren't for a dash of Angostura bitters; they add a bite

AMERICANO

1 ounce Campari
1 ounce sweet vermouth
Soda water
Orange twist for garnish

———— MAKES 1 DRINK ————

Pour the Campari, vermouth, and soda water, in that order, into an ice-filled pilsner or collins glass. Garnish with the orange twist.

and level of interest that bourbon and vermouth can't on their own. We even like to add a dash or two of orange bitters to our Manhattan because it lends an additional layer of flavor and blends beautifully with the sweet notes of bourbon. When we say a dash or two, we mean just that, because adding too much bitters to a cocktail can quickly ruin the drink.

While their number and range of style are not nearly as great as they were during the beginning of the last century, there are still a few bitters that make wonderful assets behind any bar, including yours. Thanks to their digestive qualities as well as their ability to wake up an appetite, they are good in both aperitif- and digestif-style cocktails.

The most widely available of its kind, Angostura bitters impart an exotically dry and herbal quality to everything from a Champagne cocktail to an **OLD-FASHIONED**. Peychaud's bitters are still made with the recipe that was developed by Antoine Peychaud, a nineteenth-century Creole pharmacist. They are not only essential when mixing a true **SAZERAC** but also make a great addition to cocktails featuring brown spirits, such as brandy or bourbon. Sweeter than other bitters, Peychaud's tends to bring out some of the caramel-like qualities in these spirits. Originally a staple in countless cocktail recipes, orange bitters are now difficult to find, but they are worth the hunt. Dash them into a **MARTINI,** for example, and the spirit of orange zest and spice will wake up this classic cocktail.

Another category of bitters to consider when dreaming up new recipes is the potable bitters that are often poured as digestifs, such as Fernet Branca, Amaro Averna, and even Campari. When treated like any other bitters, a dash or two of these will add new layers of flavor to many stirrings. If you haven't found a good source for bitters near you, try visiting Fee Brothers or Buffalo Trace on the Internet (feebrothers.com or buffalotrace.com).

NEGRONI

1½ ounces Junipero gin

¾ ounce Campari

¾ ounce sweet vermouth, preferably Punt e Mes

1 piece orange zest with some pith, about 1½ inches long and ½ inch wide

——— MAKES 1 DRINK ———

Combine all the liquid ingredients in an ice-filled cocktail shaker. Stir gently for 20 to 30 seconds, until cold, and then strain into a chilled cocktail glass. Flame the orange zest over the drink (see page 75) and float it on top.

Dr. Schwartz's Cherry-Vanilla Bitters

BITTERS ARE NOT MADE OVERNIGHT. It takes time to gather all of the ingredients you need, and then the actual process can take weeks. When you set out to make your own bitters, remember that the experimental journey can be just as interesting and enjoyable as the final product. Much of the fun involves the daily ritual of giving a jar containing quassia (from the heartwood and bark of tropical trees) or cherry bark, or other exotic ingredients a good shake and watching the liquid inside darken and intensify. You can even taste the liquid every day to see how the flavor is progressing.

The recipe below, which Rob (aka Dr. Schwartz) developed, is based on a formula, and it can be adapted to make a variety of bitters. Let your imagination run wild and dream up flavors that you think would be the perfect complement to your own cocktail creations.

Why cherry-vanilla bitters? The flavors work nicely together, and when added to a drink they do not overly sweeten it. Try using Dr. Schwartz's bitters as a substitute for your regular bitters in virtually any cocktail recipe.

DR. SCHWARTZ'S CHERRY-VANILLA BITTERS

2 teaspoons quassia (see NOTE)

2 teaspoons cardamom seeds

1½ teaspoons anise seeds

Pinch of gentian (see NOTE)

Pinch of cassia (see NOTE)

1 teaspoon grated ginger

3 cups 100 proof rye,
preferably Rittenhouse

5 vanilla beans

½ cup cherry bark

3 cups water

——————— MAKES 6 CUPS ———————

Toast the quassia, cardamom, anise, gentian, and cassia in a dry frying pan over medium heat for a few minutes until fragrant. Cool, and transfer to a sterile mason jar. Add the ginger and rye, screw on the cap, shake well, and store in a cool, dark place. Agitate once a day for one week. Strain the mixture through cheesecloth and transfer to a clean jar. Gather the ends of the cheesecloth to squeeze out as much liquid as possible.

Cut the vanilla beans in half lengthwise and add them to the rye mixture along with the cherry bark. Seal and store again, shaking once a day, for another 2 weeks. Strain the rye through cheesecloth and transfer to a clean mason jar (do not throw out the cherry and vanilla mash). Cover and set aside for a couple of weeks. (No need to agitate.)

Take the cherry-vanilla mash remaining in the jar and transfer to a medium saucepan. Add the 3 cups of water and bring to boil. Reduce the heat and simmer for 20 minutes. While the mixture is simmering, smash the vanilla beans against the sides of the pot with a muddler or wooden spoon. Cool completely and transfer to a clean jar. Store in a cool, dark place for another 2 weeks, agitating once daily. Strain this mixture through several layers of cheesecloth, as many times as is necessary to remove all sediment from the vanilla beans. Finally, combine the liquid with the reserved rye mixture and transfer to an empty bitters bottle.

NOTE: You can order quassia, gentian, and cassia from Tenzing Momo, on the Web at tenzingmomo.com.

SINGAPORE SLING

2 ounces gin

¾ ounce cherry brandy,
preferably Cherry Heering

2 teaspoons Bénédictine

2 ounces pineapple juice

¾ ounce fresh lime juice

2 dashes grenadine

Dash of Angostura bitters

Soda water

3 brandied cherries (PAGE 76)
for garnish

Orange slice for garnish

———— MAKES 1 DRINK ————

Combine the gin, brandy, Bénédictine, juices, grenadine, and bitters in an ice-filled cocktail shaker. Shake until cold, and then strain into an ice-filled collins glass. Top with soda water and garnish with the cherries and orange slice.

THIS RECIPE COMES DIRECTLY FROM THE RAFFLES HOTEL IN SINGAPORE, WHERE THE DRINK WAS CREATED IN 1915.

La Fée Verte
(The Green Fairy)

WHEN BILL RUSSELL-SHAPIRO looked for inspiration for his new brasserie in San Francisco, he went further back in time than the Prohibition period to France's turn-of-the-century Belle Epoque, a period of innovation in art and architecture. Eager to call to mind the essence of this era, especially in Paris, he chose the name Absinthe.

If we could wander the streets of Paris during that period, we'd find a city perfumed by the lingering aroma of anise, the predominant flavor of absinthe. This highly alcoholic and bitter liquor entranced the French with its cloudy green mystique and intoxicating effects. It was distilled from numerous herbs and spices, the most important being the plant wormwood, which, when distilled, releases the narcotic component thujone. Wormwood is known scientifically as *Artemisia absinthium;* the French word for it is "absinthe." It has a devilishly bitter taste when consumed on its own, and legends linking this bitterness with evil go back to biblical times.

Artists such as Vincent Van Gogh and Henri Toulouse-Lautrec drank it in copious amounts and immortalized it in their art. Nearly every night during the late 1800s, cafés in Paris would play host to l'heure verte ("the green hour"). Between the hours of about six and seven, a majority of cafés in the city would fill with crowds eager to experience the illusory world of the green fairy (la fée verte).

Absinthe was regarded as a cure-all herbal tonic, as well as an inebriant. By the early 1900s, however, suspicions began to arise that it had the power to land the imbiber in an asylum because of its extraordinarily high alcohol content—which could be as much as 75 to 80 percent, or 150 to 160 proof—and the mind-altering qualities of thujone. Consideration was almost never given to the fact that most of the absinthe drunk during that time was made from alcohol containing enough impurities to kill a horse! The cheapest and therefore most heavily consumed absinthes were full of these harmful components.

The declining public view of absinthe plunged further when on August 28, 1905, a Swiss man murdered his wife and child and then tried to take his own life. Following the murders, it was found that the man had drunk two glasses of absinthe earlier that day. Despite the fact that he'd also consumed other alcohols the same afternoon, absinthe was blamed as the source of his actions. This incident was a primary catalyst for the eventual ban of absinthe in many countries around the world.

Today absinthe is seeing a strong resurgence around the globe. With the formation of a unified European economy, restrictions on the production and sale of absinthe have gradually been abandoned in more and more countries. Now it is possible to go online and purchase absinthe from France, Spain, the Czech Republic, and Switzerland, among others. Bottles of the spirit can be legally shipped to the States; they just can't be resold once they're here. Absinthe is attracting a growing counter-cultural movement of people hoping to experience the loopy and mildly hallucinogenic buzz that only thujone can provide. The movement is growing so quickly that even the first commercial producer of the spirit, Pernod, has once again begun to distill absinthe from what it believes is its original recipe.

The question remains, does absinthe make you crazy? It is safe to assume that the methods of yesteryear that were used to test the harmfulness of absinthe wouldn't measure up to today's standards. Considering the limited amount of thujone found in a glass of absinthe (especially after it's been diluted with water), it is probably safe to say that the most harmful part of absinthe lies in its high alcohol content, since absinthes produced today are much cleaner and freer of the older, more harmful poisons. So if it is approached with moderation and respect, we believe absinthe could be considered as safe as almost any other aperitif.

FRENCH 75

½ ounce Simple Syrup (PAGE 116)

½ ounce fresh lemon juice

1½ ounces gin

Champagne

3 brandied cherries (PAGE 76) for garnish

Lemon twist for garnish

———— MAKES 1 DRINK ————

In an ice-filled pilsner or collins glass, combine the syrup, lemon juice, and gin, and stir to mix. Fill the glass to the top with Champagne and garnish with the cherries and lemon twist.

THIS RECIPE COMES FROM *LIFE IN THE TRENCHES* BY HAROLD SANDERS, 1919.

A GLOSSARY OF DRINKS

BUCK
A highball with lime juice added.

CHILLER
A highball made with ginger ale.

COBBLER
A base spirit or wine stirred with sugar, poured over crushed ice, and garnished with plenty of seasonal fruit.

COCKTAIL
According to tradition, spirit, bitters, and sugar stirred or shaken and served up.

COLLINS
Lemon juice, a spirit, sugar, and soda.

COOLER
Similar to a crusta, with the addition of soda.

CRUSTA
A drink garnished with the entire zest of a lemon or orange, served in a glass that is "crusted" with sugar.

DAISY
A sour with raspberry syrup or grenadine.

FIX
A sour with pineapple syrup.

FIZZ
A drink made with a spirit, syrup or sugar, lime or lemon juice, and egg white.

FLIP
Wine or sherry shaken with sugar and a whole egg; it can be served hot or cold.

FRAPPE (also called a mist)
Any single spirit served on crushed ice.

GOLDEN FIZZ
A fizz shaken with the yolk of an egg.

HIGHBALL
Any single spirit and carbonated mixer over ice.

JULEP
A spirit, mint, and sugar served over crushed ice.

MULL
Wine, spices, and sugar served hot.

POSSET
Sweetened and spiced milk served hot with a spirit.

POUSSE CAFÉ
Liquors floated on top of one another to create a rainbow of taste and flavor.

PUNCH
Spirits, water, and sugar flavored with fruits. Can be served hot or cold and as an individual drink or in a large bowl.

RICKEY
A spirit, lime juice, sugar, and soda.

SANGAREE
A chilled and sweetened liquor served in a highball glass and garnished with nutmeg.

SHRUB
A premix made by infusing fruits or fruit juices, sugar, and spirits; the premix is then added to any carbonated mixer.

SLING
A spirit, sugar, bitters, and lemon juice served over ice.

SMASH
A spirit, mint, sugar, and lemon juice served over ice.

SOUR
A spirit, sugar, and lemon or lime juice.

SQUIRT
A spirit, fruit syrup, and soda.

SWIZZLE
A sour stirred with a swizzle stick until the outside of the glass frosts.

TODDY
A spirit and water, most often hot, with sugar, citrus, and spices.

candied ginger
syrup = 1oz

Ginger Rogers

Havana Ra

jamaican rum
Parfait
amour
ahisette
grenadine

(Inside
Secrets)

ON ANY GIVEN DAY

ON THE CORNER OF HAYES AND GOUGH,
WE SERVE AFTERNOON SHOPPERS, PRE-THEATER DINERS,
POST-SHOW DRINKERS, AND LATE NIGHT NIBBLERS.

FROM OUR VANTAGE

BEHIND THE BAR,

WE WATCH DAYS AND NIGHTS GO BY
AS PEOPLE STOP IN AND
BELLY-UP TO THE COPPER BAR.

2

OUR PROXIMITY TO THE OPERA, SYMPHONY, AND THE HAYES VALLEY boutiques has always produced waves of guests coming and going through our doors. During the mad pre-performance rush, when the number of guests in the bar and restaurant goes from 15 to 150 within a matter of minutes, or when a sudden downpour brings hordes of shoppers in for a lingering drink and a dozen oysters while they dry out, we hardly have time to think, let alone spend time chatting with guests.

As each group steps up to the bar, we offer a cocktail menu as we slide back and forth grabbing glassware, turning over bottles, muddling, and shaking. Within minutes we are asking a host for another stack of menus as the crowd becomes two and three deep. Making our way from group to group, we try to remember who was first, offering suggestions, taking orders, and assembling drinks in groups of two, four, and eight. We hear people talking about the show they've just seen, wondering aloud whether the rain will stop, and planning the coming weekend.

While we may not be able to focus on each conversation, our ears are open, listening for feedback, ready to attend to each guest's needs. And like chefs peeking through the kitchen to see a diner's response to the dish set before him, we'll put one of our creations down and wait for a customer to take the first sip.

As bartenders, we are the entertainers and hosts of the bar. We know that the art of entertaining involves always being aware of the little things, such as whether or not this person is in need of another cocktail, that person is ready to order a bite to eat, or another group is ready to settle the check. And all of this must happen during the bustle of a rush. We may look like whirling dervishes spinning around behind the bar putting together drink after drink, but we're always paying attention.

When at home, the same art of entertaining applies. You will have guests arriving and guests leaving. You may be doing your best to visit with some and wishing you had time to talk with others. The better prepared you are for your event the more time you will have to be a great host. But even if you have hired people to help, you should always keep an eye and ear on your guests to see who needs what and make sure they are enjoying what you have presented to them. You might not be able to change anything major for an upcoming party, but you might gain some valuable insights for your next one!

We love what we do, and we take pride in each cocktail passed across the bar. So when a guest likes one of our creations enough to actually stop and say, "Wow, that's good!", it makes our efforts worthwhile. By taking the time to listen to our guests and make adjustments based on their comments, we create a feeling of intimacy and comfort.

We've all been to places where the bartenders slam out the drinks like fast food, knowing that there will be other guests along who will gladly accept whatever they are served. By mastering the simple art of listening, we're able to cater to each guest's desires. If you hear someone comment to a friend that her cocktail is too sweet, adjust the next one or suggest another drink that may be better suited to her tastes until you've achieved the drink she desires. Guests will always appreciate your role as the host when you take a few extra moments to truly understand their needs.

GINGER ROGERS

8 to 12 mint leaves
½ ounce Ginger Syrup (PAGE 119)
1½ ounces gin
½ ounce fresh lime juice
Ginger ale
Lime wedge for garnish

——————— MAKES 1 DRINK ———————

Put the mint leaves in a pilsner or a collins glass, cover with the syrup, and muddle lightly until the mint begins to release its aroma. Fill the glass with ice and add the gin and lime juice. Top with the ginger ale. Using a bar spoon, stir the drink from the bottom up to mix. Garnish with the lime wedge.

CREATED BY FORMER ABSINTHE BAR MANAGER, MARCOVALDO DIONYSOS.

HAVANA

1½ ounces Gosling's rum

¾ ounce Cointreau

½ ounce fresh lime juice

¼ ounce Simple Syrup (PAGE 116)

Splash of orange juice

Dash of orange bitters

——————— MAKES 1 DRINK ———————

Combine all the ingredients in an ice-filled cocktail shaker. Shake until cold, and then strain into a sugar-rimmed cocktail glass. If available, garnish with edible flowers.

THE IMPORTANCE OF QUALITY

BY THE TIME ABSINTHE FIRST OPENED ITS DOORS IN 1998, the country was showing a rejuvenated thirst for the cocktail. This growing movement brought with it one unexpected and lasting change: Patrons were interested not only in cocktails but also in high-quality specialty spirits. Suddenly there was an incredible surge in brand loyalty that was probably directly related to the explosion in brand marketing, as exemplified by the early master of this business, Absolut. By the time Absinthe served its first guests, the general drinking public was certainly geared up for the top-quality cocktails the bar had to offer.

Marcovaldo Dionysos, Absinthe's first bar manager and creator of our most popular cocktail, the **GINGER ROGERS,** wanted to demonstrate that the experience of sipping a cocktail was vastly improved when the sweet, processed mixes that had become staples during the '70s and '80s were replaced with fresh juices and carefully prepared seasonal syrups. Following the lead of the bartenders of yesteryear, he dug up recipes from century-old cocktail books and developed a drink list of well-made potions built with quality ingredients and fashioned in the style enjoyed during the golden age of cocktails.

While Marco was perfecting his drinks, the restaurant world was changing. Chefs were becoming superstars, composing seasonal ingredients of the highest quality into works of art. Superior cocktails, and the bartenders who created them, were poised and ready to make their own grand entrance onto the restaurant scene. More and more, top-quality bars and restaurants like Absinthe were taking lessons from history by squeezing fresh juices and making syrups from scratch. Throughout the 1990s, as the cocktail world worked its way back toward its roots, it became clear to professional and home bartenders alike that the only way to end up with an authentic, top-quality drink was to start by using top-quality ingredients.

BATTLE OF NEW ORLEANS

1½ ounces bourbon
3 dashes Peychaud's bitters
Dash of Herbsaint
Dash of orange bitters
Dash of anisette
Lemon twist for garnish

——— MAKES 1 DRINK ———

Combine all the liquid ingredients in an ice-filled cocktail shaker. Stir gently for 20 to 30 seconds, until cold, and then strain into a chilled cocktail glass. Garnish with the lemon twist.

RECIPE ADAPTED FROM *THE STANDARD COCKTAIL GUIDE* BY CROSBY GAIGE, 1944.

GOOD SPIRITS, FRESH JUICES, AND APPEALING GARNISHES

IN MOST CASES, NO MATTER WHAT TYPE OF COCKTAIL you are going to be assembling, the main or base ingredient is going to be a spirit—be it vodka, gin, rum, bourbon, Scotch, brandy, or tequila. When considering the spirit, the first thing you should think about is quality. Contrary to popular belief, it isn't necessary to go for the most expensive spirit in each category every time you shop. In fact, the most expensive spirits, especially brandies, bourbons, Scotches, and tequilas, are artisanal and often are meant to be sipped without embellishment. This doesn't mean that they can't be used in cocktails. On the contrary, many of these spirits tend to be older and more developed, meaning they can lend subtle nuances of sweetness or spice to the right cocktail. Just keep in mind that the cost of using ultra-premium spirits in cocktails can add up quickly; you might want to reserve them for the most important occasions.

While we advise against going all-out for the most expensive spirits when building your bar, we'd also like to point out that it's best not to go for the cheapest spirits, either. When you start with a spirit that doesn't taste good on its own, you end up looking to the other ingredients to mask a negative flavor, and in most cases what you end up with is a muddy mess of a drink. Besides, cheaper-quality spirits tend to have a higher concentration of sugars, creating a sweetness that helps to mask imperfections in the distilling process, and those sugars are also incredible hangover generators. If you start with a base spirit that actually tastes good, then the role of the other ingredients used in the cocktail should be to enhance the base. The goal is to create a drink that tastes better than each ingredient on its own.

A cocktail comprises a base spirit that is mixed with other ingredients. So once you've decided on which spirits you want to feature in your bar, it is time to consider the other ingredients that are going into the shaker.

Here again, whether someone is mixing drinks professionally or at home for a few friends, quality is of the utmost importance.

A good number of cocktails call for some form of juice, the most common being lime or lemon. We can't stress enough the importance of using freshly squeezed juices—the difference between fresh and artificial juices is one that can make or break your cocktail. If you are going to take shortcuts, this is not the place to start. Fresh juice is vibrant and bright, and it helps a cocktail to dance on your palate. If a cocktail could be described as life in a glass, then fresh juice is its blood.

AVIATION

2 ounces gin
1 ounce fresh lemon juice
2 dashes maraschino liqueur
Lime wedge for garnish

——— MAKES 1 DRINK ———

In an ice-filled cocktail shaker, combine the gin, lemon juice, and maraschino liqueur. Shake until cold, and then strain into a chilled cocktail glass. Garnish with the lime wedge.

PADDLE BOAT

1 ounce bourbon
½ ounce fresh orange juice
½ ounce Mathilde framboise
½ ounce white crème de cacao
3 raspberries for garnish

——————— MAKES 1 DRINK ———————

Combine all the liquid ingredients in an ice-filled cocktail shaker. Shake until cold, and then strain into a chilled cocktail glass. Garnish with the raspberries.

If you squeeze fresh juice in advance, always keep it in airtight bottles and refrigerate when not in use in order to keep it from going sour. Also, remember that pulp can get messy and interfere with the final appearance of your cocktail, so straining citrus juices is always advised. It will also make cleaning those glasses a whole lot easier.

Fruit purées have recently become extremely common in bars throughout the country. Passion fruit, mango, pear, or melon—just about any type of fruit can be cut up and blended into a purée. If you decide to work with purées, remember to keep them in the fridge or freezer—they spoil very quickly and have been known to ruin a cocktail or two.

Garnishes are an integral part of the cocktail and should be treated with the same respect as any other ingredient. If you are going to the trouble of using the best ingredients in your drinks, don't skimp on the quality of your garnishes. It is important to remember that the way a cocktail is perceived before that first sip is taken affects how it will be received. If you add a dried-out sliver of lemon, or a wedge of lime that is brown along the edges, your guest is likely to anticipate a listless cocktail, and you are probably better off adding no garnish at all. A garnish is the cocktail's finishing touch that brings all the other ingredients together.

In addition to base spirits, juices, and garnishes, your other ingredients should be of top quality, too. If a recipe calls for egg whites or cream, then by all means use the freshest you can find and be sure to properly store. You wouldn't use old eggs in your Caesar salad dressing, so why would you want to use them in a cocktail? If you add spices, make sure they are fresh. Use freshly grated nutmeg whenever possible.

Be sure to taste each ingredient on its own before adding it to the finished cocktail; that way you don't have to work backwards trying to figure out who spoiled the party. This is also a good habit to get into because it gives you an idea of how each ingredient works in the drink, and helps you balance them.

The main reason always to use the highest-quality ingredients, of course, is that your guests will notice a difference in the cocktails you serve.

Base Spirits

brandy

At its most basic, brandy is the simple term for any spirit that is distilled from a fruit, its juice, or its pulp; it's often aged in wood. The term "brandy" derives from the Dutch word *brandewijn,* or "burnt wine." It refers to the ancient distillation practice of heating a fermented liquid with a flame in order to vaporize and reconstitute the alcohol. What is typically referred to today as brandy is a spirit made from grapes and aged in oak barrels for anywhere from two years to forty or more in the case of the most elegant versions. Cognac, produced in the Charentes region of France, is by far the most famous brandy in the world, but world-class brandies are also produced in other areas of France, most notably Armagnac and Calvados, where the brandy is produced from apples. Brandy is produced in just about every country in the world from all types of fruit.

gin

We think of gin as the ultimate cocktail spirit. It is the base for the quintessential MARTINI, it stands strong with the bitter undertones in a NEGRONI, and its aromatic flavors lend depth to any number of other creations. Originating in Holland, gin is a grain (typically wheat or rye) spirit that is the product of a double-distillation process. The first distillation produces a neutral spirit that weighs in at 96 percent alcohol by volume, or 192 proof! During the second, the spirit is distilled with juniper berries and a variety of other botanicals which give gin its distinctive flavor. Recipes vary depending upon the style of gin that the producer desires. Common botanicals include coriander seed, angelica, dried lemon and orange peel, licorice, cassia bark, cardamom, and even cinnamon. After completing the second distillation, the producer reduces gin to a bottling strength of about 80 proof by diluting it with water.

rum

Rum is distilled from molasses, sugarcane juice, cane syrup, or raw sugarcane. Agricultural rum was once referred to as "kill devil," either because its perceived medicinal qualities could ward off ills brought on by the devil, or because the rums produced in New England during the early days of colonization were so impure that they could even kill the devil. Whatever the case, rum was *the* spirit of the New World, and it had direct ties to both the English and American slave trade that would last for more than 200 years. Today rum is a versatile spirit; it is aged for a minimum of one year in an oak barrel to make silver rums, and for three years or more to make dark rums. While silver rums tend to lend themselves to tropics-driven and citrus-based cocktails, aged rums are at home in more complex pairings with ingredients like sherry and rich, sweet vermouths. Or they can be sipped on their own.

tequila

This Mexican spirit is double-distilled from a plant scientifically known as *Agave tequilana,* more commonly known as the blue-agave plant, which is related to the lily family. Like Cognac and Scotch, tequila has a denomination of origin regulated by the Mexican government. By law there are only five states in Mexico that may produce tequila, and only blue agave spirits coming from one of these states may legally be labeled *tequila.* The spirit can be broken down into two primary categories: those made

from 100 percent blue agave, and those made from a mixture of blue agave and additional sugars known as *mixtos.* From here, tequila can be categorized further by its age classification, the most important being *blanco, reposado,* and *añejo. Blanco,* or silver, tequilas are not aged and are typically bottled directly after the tequila's second distillation. *Reposado,* or rested, tequilas are aged for less than one year in a barrel. *Añejo,* or aged, tequilas spend at least one year in an oak barrel, and some premium tequilas rest for over four years.

whiskey

Whether it is spelled with the "e" as we do here in the States, or without, as they do in Scotland, "whiskey" is the generic term for a distilled grain spirit that is aged in a wood barrel. The word is thought to originate from the Gaelic term *uisquebaugh,* meaning "water of life."

scotch

Distilled from barley and cooked over peat fires, Scotch is a true spirit delight. The flavor varies, depending on the region where it is produced. Scotch can be light and fruity when it comes from the warmer Lowlands of Scotland, and filled with intense flavors of peat, smoke, and brine when it is from the island of Islay. In the Highlands, Scotland's largest whiskey-producing district, the spirit can be a combination of the two types, depending on the producer, location, and type of terrain. By law, Scotch must be aged in oak barrels for a minimum of three years, though most are aged for considerably longer. A Scotch that is labeled "single malt" comes from only one distillery.

bourbon

Bourbon is distilled from a blend of fermented corn and either wheat or rye, depending on the producer. By law, bourbon must be at least 51 percent distilled corn; when it is more than 80 percent corn, it must be labeled "corn whiskey." Most bourbon producers typically use a ratio of about 70 percent corn and 30 percent other grains. If the spirit is made from more than 51 percent rye, then it is called a rye whiskey, and will usually have a spicier tone than most bourbons. Like Scotch, bourbon must spend some time in an oak barrel, but there are interesting differences. While Scotch is usually aged in used bourbon barrels, bourbon must spend at least two years in new, charred American white-oak barrels. Bourbon's distinctive amber color comes from this aging process; no additive color may be used when producing the spirit. Although bourbon takes its name from Bourbon County, Kentucky, it is no longer produced there.

vodka

Vodka—a crystalline, odorless, and typically flavorless spirit—is distilled from a fermented mash of grains such as rye or wheat, as well as potatoes, sometimes beets, and even grapes. While each brand of vodka carries its own individual character, which generally comes from the water used in the distillation process, the goal of most vodka producers today is to create an odorless and virtually flavorless neutral spirit. To create this desired result, vodka is often distilled several times and subjected to a charcoal filtering process. Although the Russians have been infusing their vodkas with various fruits and spices for hundreds of years, it wasn't until the early 1980s that the concept of flavored vodkas took hold among the Western drinking population.

STOCKHOLM

1½ ounces Charbay Meyer
lemon vodka

¾ ounce fresh lemon juice

½ ounce Simple Syrup
(PAGE 116)

Splash of chilled Champagne
or another sparkling wine

——— MAKES 1 DRINK ———

In an ice-filled cocktail shaker, combine the vodka, lemon juice, and simple syrup. Shake until cold, and then strain into a sugar-rimmed cocktail glass. Top with the Champagne.

MINT JULEP

1 sugar cube

5 to 6 mint leaves,
plus 1 more for garnish

2 ounces bourbon

Crushed ice

——— MAKES 1 DRINK ———

In a collins glass, muddle together the sugar, mint, and bourbon until the mint begins to release its aroma and the sugar dissolves. Fill the glass with crushed ice and stir with a bar spoon from the bottom up to mix. Fill with a bit more crushed ice and push the extra mint leaves into the ice so that they peek out of the glass like a small bouquet.

ASTORIA

1½ ounces gin

¾ ounce dry vermouth

2 dashes orange bitters

Lemon twist for garnish

——— MAKES 1 DRINK ———

Combine the gin and vermouth in an ice-filled cocktail shaker. Add the bitters, stir gently for 20 to 30 seconds, until cold, and then strain into a chilled cocktail glass. Garnish with a lemon twist.

SALTY POODLE

1 ounce silver tequila

¾ ounce fresh lime juice

½ ounce fresh grapefruit juice

½ ounce Cointreau

¼ ounce Fee Brothers falernum

Dash of crème de cassis

——— MAKES 1 DRINK ———

Combine all the ingredients in an ice-filled cocktail shaker. Shake until cold and strain into a salt-rimmed cocktail glass.

ICE: THERE IS MORE TO IT THAN YOU THINK.

THE MOST OVERLOOKED COMPONENT OF ANY COCKTAIL IS ICE. It comes in all shapes and sizes and in all different temperatures. You might ask, Isn't it true that any type of ice will work in a cocktail? In a pinch, yes. But ice actually serves more than one purpose, and a discerning bartender understands which type to use.

Of course we use ice to make drinks ice-cold and palatable, but its other main function is to add water to a cocktail. Water makes up as much as one-third of a cocktail. It helps to dilute the alcoholic heat built up in a drink and it also integrates some of the softer, more floral nuances found in different spirits.

A key part of making a perfectly balanced cocktail is adding the right amount of water, and this is easier to do with the right type of ice. The size dictates how much or how little water you are adding to a cocktail. Regardless of whether you are stirring or shaking, the larger the cubes or lumps the longer the ice takes to dissolve. Turn-of-the-century bartenders knew this, and they understood how different shapes and sizes of ice affect any given cocktail. Some of them even specified the size of ice in their recipes, which varied with the type of drink they were making and the amount of water they wanted to add to the drink.

Period drink recipes generally called for one of four types of ice: *block ice* was an oversized chunk that melted slowly and served as a perfect chilling agent in large punch bowls. Generally, bartenders obtained each of the smaller forms of ice from a block of ice with the help of a variety of tools. *Lump* or *cube ice* were smaller clumps that were used to chill short drinks, such as the **OLD-FASHIONED**. *Cracked ice* was achieved by breaking up lump ice cubes and worked perfectly for chilling cocktails that were to be shaken or stirred and then strained into a cocktail glass. *Snow* was ice shaved from a block and used in much the same way that we'd use crushed ice today. It worked especially well in drinks like the **MINT JULEP**.

Today most ice found in bars and restaurants comes from a machine, while homemade ice is typically made in ice-cube trays. A machine is a more efficient and cost-effective way to get ice and a great way to speed up service.

Most commercial machines make ice in the form of thin, wafer-like disks or small, hollowed-out cubes. Both of these tend to dissolve more quickly than the larger cubes found in the typical home bar. To a professional bartender, this means bartending is never a passive activity. We are constantly aware of the rate at which ice is melting when we're shaking and stirring cocktails. Shake or stir for too long and we're serving a limp, watered-down cocktail. At home, where you use larger ice cubes, the opposite is true: you must make sure that you've shaken or stirred the cocktail long enough to properly chill and dilute the drink; this takes 30 seconds or more in many cases.

Any cocktail served over ice is best shaken or stirred with smaller pieces of ice, and then poured over larger cubes. The smaller ice melts more quickly, adding water to the drink, while the larger cubes melt more slowly, keeping the drink cool. At Absinthe, if a drink is poured over ice after it has been shaken or stirred, we always provide fresh ice in the serving glass, providing a cocktail that is perfect from the first to the last sip.

When you are having a large party at home, you will need a lot of ice cubes. Consider the number of people you're expecting and calculate the number of drinks you anticipate serving. A good rule is one drink per person per hour. Make sure the vessel in your icemaker is full or start freezing those ice cubes, but remember that when the ice sits exposed in the freezer for extended periods of time, it picks up flavors from your frozen foods.

You can store the ice cubes you've made in zipper-top freezer bags. If you think you'll need still more ice, then buy bags the day you plan to entertain. Keep in mind that ice is almost always the first thing to be depleted at a party. How many times have you been to a shindig where someone yells, "We're out of ice!"? In fact, ice is the perfect thank-you item for that friend who always wants to add a contribution to your festivities.

Use your homemade ice cubes for cocktails; they can be cracked into perfectly sized pieces for shaking and stirring cocktails. Use the bagged ice for serving sodas and even simple drinks like vodka tonics so you don't burn through your homemade ice too quickly. Remember to keep your ice dry and cold by leaving it in the freezer until needed. Ice that sits around at room temperature melts too fast in the shaker and glasses, leaving watery cocktails.

You can also make blocks of ice to keep sodas, juices, and beer cold in ice chests. Simply freeze water in large plastic containers; then run a bit of hot water around the outside of the containers to release the block.

When making punch, the bigger the ice the better. Think of the punch bowl as one giant cocktail. Cubes that are the correct size for a glass would be minuscule in a large punch bowl, and melt very fast. The nature of a bowl of punch is to sit around for hours, and the ice is there to keep the liquid cold while adding as little additional water as possible. Should your guests want to drink their punch on the rocks, keep a small bucket of ice by the punch bowl.

Home ice-cube trays come in all kinds of sizes and shapes. Experiment to see which works best for each type of cocktail. You can break the bigger cubes into different sizes of cracked ice. Just take a few cubes, wrap them in a clean bar- or dish-towel, and either smack them on the counter or use a mallet. It is possible to make crushed ice by filling a cocktail shaker with cracked ice or cubes and mashing them vigorously with a muddler or the back of a wooden spoon. If you want to wow all of your friends with your creative touch, decorate the ice blocks and cubes by freezing colorful fruits and flowers in them.

CAN YOU MAKE ME A PIÑA COLADA?

YOU MAY NOTICE WHEN THUMBING THROUGH THE PAGES of this book that there are no recipes that call for the use of a blender. This is not an oversight. Our focus at Absinthe has always been on the cocktail classics, and in our view blended drinks tend to be more gimmicky than anything else. Typically, these umbrella-clad concoctions use hypersweet mixes and too much ice, and are best consumed while floating in a pool on a cruise ship in the South Pacific. Besides, we couldn't imagine the whirring din of an electric blender shattering Absinthe's dining room dinner conversation.

Despite these beliefs, we are aware that blended drinks can be a popular and festive choice, given the right situation. Hell, we've even been guilty of pulling out a blender once or twice at parties in order to whip together a few of our own "boat" drinks. If you do find yourself at a party reaching for a blender, remember that it is still important to use fresh, good-quality ingredients. Instead of reaching for overly sweet frozen-fruit mixes, try freezing fresh fruit and then tossing it in the blender along with your desired booze. By doing this, you not only avoid the artificial flavors that are too often found in most frozen drink mixes, but you also reduce the amount of ice you're putting into your drink. The frozen fruit will double as ice cubes. If the frozen fruit isn't as sweet as you'd like, gradually add a bit of simple syrup until you achieve the desired sweetness.

After raiding the freezer at parties, we've discovered that gourmet sorbets are great for adding hard-to-find or out-of-season fruit flavors to all sorts of boat drinks. If it's late, and you're in the mood for a cocktail that can double as dessert, try blending your favorite boutique ice cream or gelato into a cocktail for milkshake-y creaminess.

When you're entertaining, keep in mind that sometimes the best parties are the ones that lead you down an unexpected path. Never mind that you wanted to make classic Hemingway-style **DAIQUIRIS** and **MARGARITAS** for your summer clambake; there's always the chance that someone will expect to see a blender on the bar. When that person does speak up, challenge and surprise those preconceived ideas by whipping up something fresh, creative, and out of their world.

TO SHAKE OR STIR? THAT IS THE QUESTION.

THE ARGUMENT OVER WHETHER A COCKTAIL SHOULD BE shaken or stirred is almost as old as the cocktail itself. Well, maybe not that old, but at least to 1960's James Bond ordering his Vodka Martini "shaken, not stirred." Generally, the argument revolves around the **MARTINI,** but we've seen it carry over to other drinks, like the **MANHATTAN**.

Some say that Martinis should never be shaken because you run the risk of bruising the delicate nuances of the gin or vodka featured in the drink. Others disregard the bruising theory, and say that the only way to properly chill a cocktail, especially a Martini, is to shake it vigorously for at least 30 seconds. In their minds no amount of stirring will get the drink cold enough. To these lovers of the über-cold, a properly shaken Martini should have little flecks of ice floating on top of the drink. As for the argument over the Manhattan, there are some who stick to the "shaking means colder, and colder is better" philosophy, while others say that shaking creates foam on top of the drink, disrupting its texture. Shaking makes a cocktail opaque and sometimes opalescent, while stirring it leaves a sparkling, crystal-clear gem in the glass. Other bartenders will also stir a **MARGARITA** rather than shake it. They do this ostensibly to build the drink directly in the serving glass. If you are served one of these, you will be lucky if the ingredients are properly mixed.

So, when is it best to shake a cocktail and when is it best to stir? In a nutshell, any time a cocktail is made entirely of spirits the drink should be stirred, since all the bartender needs to do is to mix the flavors well while chilling the drink. When a cocktail has fruit juice of any kind, cream, or egg white, it should be shaken in order to completely blend the ingredients.

ROB / One of my favorite sounds in the world has to be ice cubes clinking around in a mixing glass. Stirring is an area where individual style can really come into play. I've seen bartenders who bend the end of the mixing spoon so that while they're stirring, it creates a tornado effect. I believe the twisted design of the mixing spoon is not only for looks and tradition but also for functionality. If you hold the spoon between your thumb and first two fingers, you can twist it back and forth while you plunge it up and down in the glass. What you're trying to achieve is a very steady twist and plunge. You do not have to go crazy violently stirring, or agitating so much that you are adding chips of ice or tiny air bubbles to the cocktail, which will spoil its appearance and texture. You want a silky cocktail, and when you serve a Martini or Manhattan, you want it to be crystal clear.

VELVET ORANGE

(pictured left)

1 ounce Hangar 1 Mandarin Blossom vodka

¼ ounce Prime Arance orange brandy

¼ ounce fresh orange juice

¼ ounce Velvet Falernum

Splash of fresh lime juice

1 piece orange zest with some pith,
about 1½ inches long and ½ inch wide

——— MAKES 1 DRINK ———

Combine all the liquid ingredients in an ice-filled cocktail shaker. Shake until cold, and then strain into a chilled cocktail glass. Flame the orange over the drink (see page 75) and float it on top.

BRAZIL 66

1 lime, cut into wedges

¾ ounce Simple Syrup (PAGE 116)

1 ounce cachaça

½ ounce Cointreau

½ ounce fresh orange juice

Orange twist for garnish

——— MAKES 1 DRINK ———

In a pilsner or collins glass, muddle the lime with the syrup. Fill the glass with ice, and add the remaining liquid ingredients. Transfer to the mixing glass of a cocktail shaker, cover, and tap gently to ensure a strong seal, and shake well. Pour the drink back into the original glass. Garnish with the orange twist.

CREATED BY FORMER ABSINTHE BAR MANAGER, OWEN DUNN.

JITNEY JUMBLE

2 ounces Basil Hayden bourbon

½ ounce iced tea

¼ ounce Simple Syrup (PAGE 116)

¼ ounce kirsch

Dash of white crème de cacao

Orange twist for garnish

——— MAKES 1 DRINK ———

Combine all the liquid ingredients in an ice-filled cocktail shaker. Shake until cold, and then strain into a chilled cocktail glass. Garnish with the orange twist.

CREATED BY ABSINTHE BARTENDER, XAN DEVOSS.

NEVADA

1½ ounces rum

½ ounce fresh grapefruit juice

⅓ ounce fresh lime juice

¼ ounce Simple Syrup (PAGE 116)

Dash of Angostura bitters

Lime wedge for garnish

——— MAKES 1 DRINK ———

Combine all the liquid ingredients in an ice-filled cocktail shaker. Shake until cold, and then strain into a chilled cocktail glass. Garnish with the lime wedge.

THIS RECIPE IS FROM *HERE'S HOW* BY W.C. WHITFIELD, 1941.

WATER ON THE SIDE

WE HAVE A REGULAR CUSTOMER WHO COMES AND TAKES a post at Absinthe's bar for at least a few hours almost every night that we are open. Some evenings he stops in for a drink or two after a long day at the office, and other times he pops by to say hello to a bartender and winds up having dinner and staying for the rest of the evening. In fact, he comes in so often that he jokes about Absinthe being his kitchen and living room all in one, which is convenient, considering that he lives and works less than a block down the street! What we've always found most interesting about his visits, even more than their frequency, is his diligence about ordering a pint of water with every cocktail or glass of wine that he sips while at the bar. He is proud of this diligence, and frequently claims that he can drink all night if he wants to because he paces himself with glasses of water along the way.

In his case, at least, this is true. There have been many nights when he's walked in the door before another guest, sipped his drinks seemingly no faster or slower than the latecomer, and walked out seemingly steady and level-headed long after the other guest was showing the effects of his drinking. This is not to say that drinking should be looked at as a contest, but we've always been impressed with his loyalty and faith in a simple glass of water. He knows that by diluting the alcohol with water, he'll be better off at the end of the night, and won't wake up cursing himself in the morning.

Walk into most any high-end cocktail bar around the turn of the century, and your bartender would serve you a full glass of water with every cocktail. This is still the norm in Europe. At Absinthe we've always embraced the sometimes forgotten knowledge of these old-timers, and we encourage sipping water while consuming alcohol. If, after an evening of drinking, a guest's original glass of water remains untouched, we have a good idea of who will not be feeling well the next day.

Contrary to many people's misconceptions, however, drinking water, especially in large amounts at the end of the night, won't help you to sober up any faster. At this point, the booze is already in your system. But that doesn't mean that avoiding water altogether is the right way to go. Remember, alcohol dehydrates, which means that it causes your body to lose more water than it normally would. Your liver, which does the majority of the work when it comes to removing alcohol from your system, needs water to do its job effectively, and it is frequently forced to pull supplies of water from other organs, including your brain—hangover, anyone? By alternating between water and

booze when you're at a bar or a party, you're helping prevent your body from drying out too severely and lending a helping hand to your well-deserving liver. Your head and body will thank you for this in the morning.

Drinking water throughout the night also encourages responsible drinking. So when you are having a party, play the role of the perfect host and offer your guests water to enjoy while they sample your cocktail creations. Offering is as easy as having small bottles of water readily available in an ice chest next to the beers and sodas. Or you can have a pitcher or two with glasses set up on your bar. You can make the pitchers even more enticing by adding sliced citrus fruits and berries to them. Throughout the night, you can invite your guests to help themselves to water whenever they like. By doing this, you are helping everyone to pace their consumption and letting them know that it isn't necessary to drink through the entire contents of the bar before the party ends. The cocktail experience should be enjoyable from the first drink to the last. If you can help your guests avoid waking up with a throbbing headache, they're more likely to thank you for the creativity of the libations you shared with them, rather than curse you for pouring them one last skull-blaster that sends them over the edge.

On the other hand, some guests may not want any alcohol in their drinks.

BOOZE-FREE CREATIONS

IN THE SPIRIT OF OUR COCKTAIL PHILOSOPHY, WE BELIEVE virgin drinks should be made with the highest-quality ingredients, freshest juices, and ripest fruits. If you are open to the limitless options available—an abundance of teas, juices, and the like—you may create refreshing elixirs that taste better than anything with alcohol. When people look for an interesting nonalcoholic beverage, what they usually want is a refreshing drink with a bright flavor that is highlighted by some fresh fruit or a savory herb. Many times, achieving the right balance with alcohol-free drinks is even easier than when booze is involved because you are working with more straightforward flavors. The subtle tones found in a variety of spirits are more difficult to work with.

Just because a drink lacks the octane of your favorite cocktail, don't assume that its appearance doesn't matter. On the contrary, just like the best cocktails, these drinks are assessed and perceived by the eye before they hit the palate, and they should present the same visual allure as a beautifully showcased alcoholic drink. Keep this in mind when you're planning your next party, and think about an inventive, balanced, and beautifully presented nonalcoholic drink for your guests to sample alongside the night's cocktails. If you're lucky, your nonalcoholic contribution might even become the foundation for your next great alcoholic cocktail!

JEFF / A while back, members of a wedding party celebrated their rehearsal dinner in our private dining room, and I got to bartend the event. I soon learned that a large group in the party was from Kentucky, which was reflected in their drinking preferences. For the most part, their orders were pretty straightforward: I poured a lot of Maker's Mark shots, MANHATTANS, and MINT JULEPS. It wasn't until one of the kids in attendance came and asked for something special that I had to stop and think for a moment. Here was this boy from Kentucky, no older than six or seven, looking up from the other side of the bar, eager to see what I could make him that would rival the drinks the grownups all around him were enjoying. Wanting to give him a drink that had its own flair, I put some mint into a pilsner glass, topped it with a bit of ginger syrup, and muddled away. In the end, the drink that I put in his eager hands was nothing more than a virgin adaptation of our GINGER ROGERS, but to him it looked like his dad's Mint Julep, and it was the best drink that he'd ever tasted. He went around proudly showing it off to everyone at the dinner, and

THE BREW AND THE VINE

EVEN THOUGH YOU'VE SPENT ALL WEEK PLANNING FOR the perfect cocktail party, digging out your favorite recipes, shopping for ingredients, setting up a space for shaking and stirring, and practicing your bartending techniques, there are always going to be guests who would love nothing more than a cold, refreshing beer or a nice glass of wine. Anticipating the desires of these friends is part of the art of entertaining, and you will want to have these staples on hand. Even the most elaborate cocktail bar in your town will offer at least a small selection of red and white wines, as well as a variety of beers.

At home it isn't necessary to feature a long list of wines that you'll be pouring during the night; nor do you need ten different styles of beer ready and waiting. However, it is always a good idea to have at least a bottle or two of good-quality white wine, chilled, and maybe one light and one full-bodied red available and ready to be opened. As for beer, a good option is to chill a lighter brew, say a Belgian-style wheat or a lager, and something a little heartier, like an ale. You can also let the season dictate what you have on hand—the colder months of winter tend to create a yearning for creamy stout, while during the dog days of summer nothing is more refreshing than a light and crisp pilsner.

We tend to consider ourselves experienced hosts, so we like to have these options ready and waiting at all times. You just never know when an unexpected guest is going to show up for an impromptu fiesta.

before I knew it, there were ten other kids standing in front of me asking for the same drink.

I could have gotten away with offering the little guy a Coke or even the old standby, a Shirley Temple, but I knew he wouldn't have been anywhere near as excited as he was with his special drink. He saw me take time to balance out the ingredients, and watched as I capped a straw to taste it before passing it across the bar. He knew the drink met with my approval. I wanted him to see that I took this creation seriously. It's a helpful attitude to have when you are trying to come up with fun, alcohol-free drinks. Why should kids, designated drivers, pregnant women, and anyone else who isn't drinking for one reason or another resign themselves to water, soda, and juice as their only beverage options?

We've all had times when an alcoholic drink was not a wise option, but we still wanted something festive in our glass. A good bartender or host will try to honor these wishes by giving the same attention to nonalcoholic drinks as he does to a fully loaded concoction.

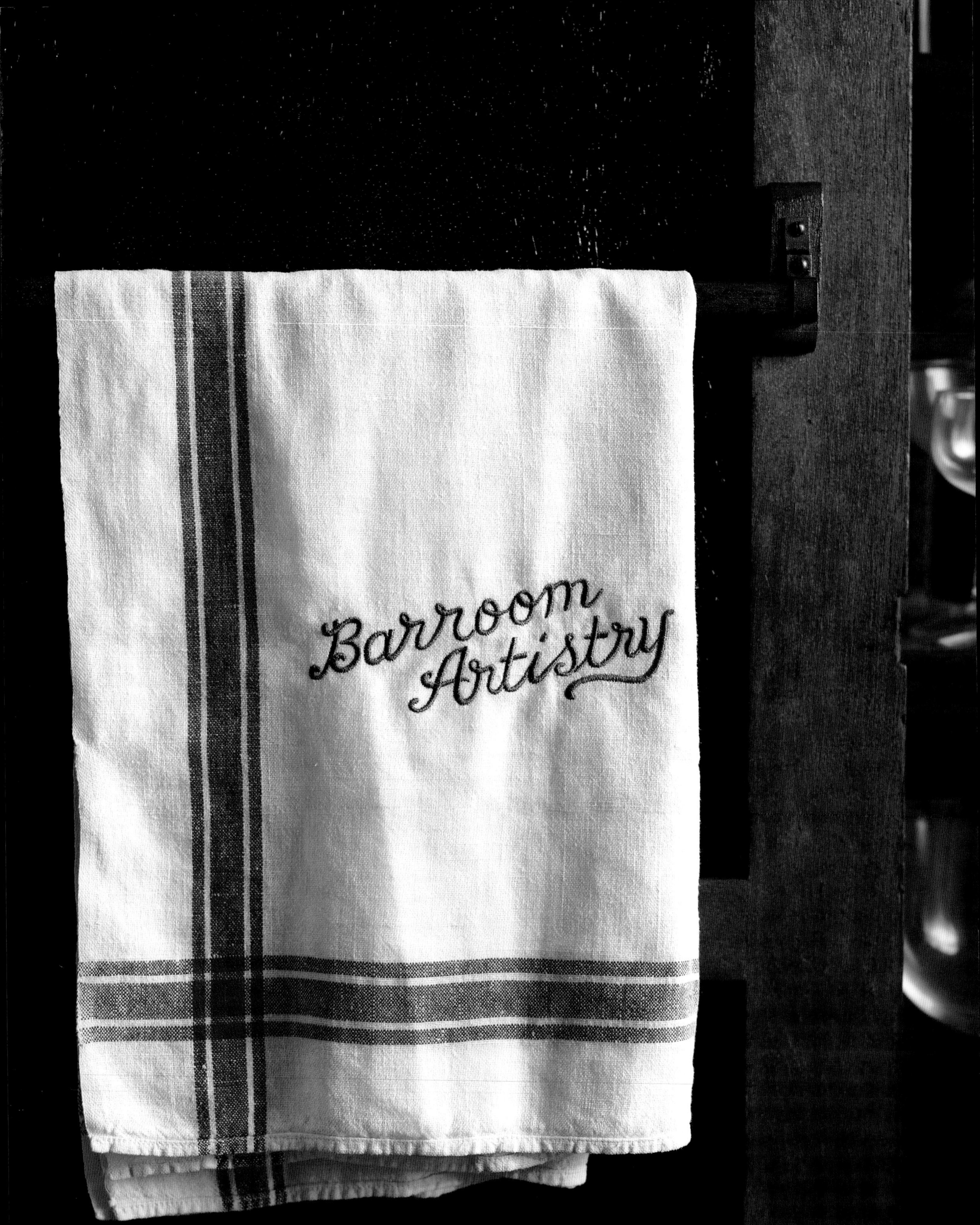
Barroom
Artistry

WHETHER WE ARE
BARTENDING AT HOME
OR AT ABSINTHE, OUR GOAL IS TO
ENTICE OUR GUESTS
WITH IMAGINATIVE, SEXY,
AND
EXQUISITELY COMPOSED
COCKTAILS.

3

AT THE BRASSERIE, A GUEST WATCHING OUR LUSCIOUS, CORAL-COLORED **PEACHES & HERB** float by on a server's tray—the drink adorned with a spectacularly ripe wedge of fresh peach and a fragrant sage leaf—is left with a lasting, mouthwatering impression. A sublime cocktail requires good-quality ingredients, well balanced liquors, and savvy presentation.

A drink's appearance can be driven by anything from unexpected glassware to the final color of the cocktail. We sometimes create a drink just so we can use an unusual garnish. In its purest form, a cocktail is a thing of beauty, seducing its recipient with its sleek and simple form. Is there anything more starkly enticing than a crystal-clear **MARTINI,** glistening in a perfectly chilled cocktail glass, with a lone olive nestled at the bottom?

Bartending artistry is also driven by a knowledge and understanding of the bartender's tools. Something as commonplace as muddling leaves of mint in a chimney glass, in order to release the herb's essence into a mojito, almost always generates an audience. So does adding a succession of spirits and bitters into a mixing glass, then attentively stirring and straining the resulting cocktail into a chilled glass. Knowing how and when to properly measure, shake, stir, muddle, build, blend, or layer your cocktails not only impresses your guests but also instills in them anticipation that you are about to present them with a glassful of something truly special.

Bounce around online, take a stroll through the bar section of any fine cookware store, or look through an antiques store's supply of vintage barware and you will be struck by the endless array of bartending gadgets, glassware, and tools from which to choose. Devotees can easily spend a lifetime, not to mention a fortune, collecting an assortment of bartending gadgets, glassware, and historical artifacts. Fortunately, if you happen to be a beginner, you really only need a few essential tools to get started: Equip yourself with a shaker, strainer, and a bar spoon, and you've got the basic tools necessary to mix most standard drinks. There are, however, a few other tools that we use often and others that, while not entirely necessary, are useful behind the bar. We've described all of these below. Your choice of glassware is limited only by your imagination and storage space.

THE COLLECTOR'S BAR

WHEN YOU SHOP FOR TOOLS AND GLASSWARE, CONSIDER YOUR taste as well as your needs. Choose tools that are functional, but that also appeal to you. If you collect antiques, you might want to look for an antique shaker, or even a martini pitcher, rather than the standard, contemporary two-piece Boston shaker. Or maybe you have some treasures in the attic, waiting to be displayed. Before you know it, you may have an entire bar collection.

You may decide to showcase the glasses that you inherited from your grandparents in a bar designed from an antique telephone booth. Or you may want to show off an array of designer crystal glassware and stylishly designed tools in a mahogany hutch. Regardless of where your tastes may lead you, a collection deserves to be celebrated. Whether you prefer to collect modern representations with sleek lines and stylish designs, or you're the type who is always looking for old-timey barware at the local antiques shop, your bar can be a reflection of your creative spirit—show it off!

GLASSWARE

THERE ARE LITERALLY HUNDREDS OF STYLES OF GLASSWARE available on the market. You'll find everything from the classic V-shaped cocktail glass to any number designed for specific drinks, such as Zombies, Hurricanes, or Irish Coffees. There are even glasses for serving every type of spirit from Cognac to single malt whiskey to vodka.

Too often a cocktail book will instruct you to start with a particular glass. While it may not be stated overtly, the suggestion is that if you don't have the proper glassware, the cocktail can't be made correctly. There may be some glassware-elitists out there who feel this way, but we're not among them. We recognize that a properly made cocktail will taste just the same served in a mason jar as it will in a crystal martini glass. Ultimately, what's important are the contents and whether or not you like the presentation. You are the artist. It's your show.

When we look for a glass in which to serve a new cocktail at the restaurant, our choices are frequently limited by what we're able to stock behind the bar. We may reach for a champagne flute in order to signal something out of the ordinary, when what we really wanted to use was a colorfully decorated antique claret glass. At home, on the other hand, you have more options. You can shop for glasses that represent your individual style and that you will be proud to display prominently in your bar. We do recommend that when choosing glasses you consider their size. The tendency is to think that bigger is better, but if a guest is casually sipping a drink in a large glass, the drink won't remain long in its icy prime. A smaller glass allows the cocktail to stay chilled until the last drop.

When choosing glassware, don't get bogged down by the conventional. Sure, you'll probably want to have a few traditional martini glasses, some version of a long glass, such as a collins or a highball glass, and something in which to serve rocks and short drinks. But they needn't all be the same style, nor should they be the only glasses that you reach for when you're making drinks. It's always exciting to be presented with a familiar cocktail in an unfamiliar manner. This can be as simple as serving your **MARTINIS** in a bucket-style glass instead of a typical cocktail glass. Just think, your guests might thank you at the end of the night because they didn't spend it trying not to spill their drink over the sides of the glass!

COCKTAIL / Also known as a martini glass. It usually holds between 4 and 8 ounces. Typically it has thin sides, so that the glass chills quickly, and a stem to keep fingers from warming the drink, since ice is almost never used in a cocktail glass.

 COLLINS / Also known as a highball glass. A collins usually ranges between 8 and 10 ounces, and can be as large as 14 ounces. Typically tall and thin, it is designed for holding ice, a base spirit, and soda. Its slender design helps to hold the fizz of the soda.

 ROCKS / Also known as a small or short glass, and ranging between 3 and 6 ounces. Generally short and squat, it is designed for holding ice and a single spirit. Sometimes a rocks glass is used for cocktails such as an **OLD-FASHIONED** or a **SAZERAC**.

 OLD-FASHIONED / Also known as a bucket glass. Short with a thick base, it is sturdy enough for muddling ingredients directly in the glass. An old-fashioned ranges between 6 and 8 ounces; larger sizes are sometimes used for serving a basic spirit and soda, or spirit and juice cocktails.

 CHAMPAGNE FLUTE / This tall, slender stemmed glass is designed to hold Champagne's bead for an extended period. Sometimes tulip-shaped, Champagne flutes vary in size from 6 to 10 ounces. Smaller flutes are great for serving sours and various other cocktails.

 WINEGLASSES / These stemmed glasses can vary greatly in size, depending on style. Typically, the glasses designed for red wine are larger than those intended for white, providing red wine with more breathing room in the glass. Smaller wineglasses with thick sides are also good for cocktails and for flaming sugar rims.

 PILSNER GLASS / A slender, sometimes footed glass designed for serving pilsner and other lighter-styled beers. The glasses range between 10 and 14 ounces and are good for serving drinks with a carbonated beverage over ice.

 SNIFTER / A short, footed glass with a wide bowl and tapered mouth, designed to hold the bouquet of fine brandies. The most useful sizes are between 5 and 8 ounces. The wide bowl is designed to allow the heat of your hand gently to warm the spirit, which releases the brandy's aromas. We also like to use snifters for serving **HOT TODDIES** and other warm drinks.

 DELMONICO / Also referred to as a sour glass. This is a short, slender, footed glass with tapered sides. It is similar to a small champagne glass, and is usually no more than 6 ounces. It is designed for serving classic sour drinks, but is also well suited for serving any sort of strained cocktail.

 IRISH COFFEE / Sometimes called a London dock glass. Usually a short, footed mug with a small handle attached to the side, an Irish-coffee glass ranges from 8 to 10 ounces. The thick glass makes it perfectly suited for serving all sorts of hot drinks, including, of course, an Irish Coffee.

LE DÉMON VERT

1½ ounces Broker's gin

½ ounce Absente

½ ounce Velvet Falernum

½ ounce fresh lime juice

Black licorice stick for garnish

—————— MAKES 1 DRINK ——————

Combine all the liquid ingredients in an ice-filled cocktail shaker. Shake until cold, and then strain into a chilled cocktail glass. Garnish with the licorice stick.

CREATED BY FORMER ABSINTHE BARTENDER, LONNIE JENSEN.

SLEEPYHEAD

2 slices orange,
plus 1 for garnish

6 to 8 mint leaves

1½ ounces brandy

½ ounce Ginger Syrup (PAGE 119)

½ ounce fresh lemon juice

Ginger ale

—————— MAKES 1 DRINK ——————

In the bottom of a mixing glass, muddle 2 slices of the orange and the mint. Top with ice and add the brandy, syrup, and lemon juice. Shake well. Pour into an ice-filled collins glass, and top with ginger ale. Garnish with the remaining slice of orange.

ESSENTIAL TOOLS

COCKTAIL SHAKER / Next to the martini glass, the cocktail shaker is perhaps the most widely recognized symbol of the bartender's craft. Since the mid-1800s, it has been used to quickly chill and combine cocktail ingredients. Prior to the invention of the cocktail shaker, bartenders typically mixed drinks by "rolling" them from one tumbler to another. This is a method that is still useful when mixing drinks featuring ingredients that shouldn't have too much air added to them, causing them to become too frothy, for example the tomato juice in a **BLOODY MARY**.

The first cocktail shaker was probably the Boston shaker, a utilitarian two-piece set of tumblers—one glass and one steel—that fit together securely, forming a seal. It is by far our favorite version of the cocktail shaker. The mixing glass is sometimes nothing more than a traditional pint glass, but in an ideal world, it is 16 ounces of tempered perfection, able to withstand the transition between hot and cold temperatures, as well as the rigors of pounding, muddling, and shaking. It is typically used as the starting point for building shaken cocktails, since you can see all the ingredients as they are added. In addition, it is the perfect glass to use when stirring a cocktail. Though learning to create and break a seal between the two pieces takes some practice, the shaker's simple design lends itself to easy cleaning and repetitive use. Once mastered, the Boston shaker is a great mixing tool for the home or professional bartender.

Two other popular shakers for home use are the three-piece, center-pour cobbler or julep shaker and the antique-style pitcher or teapot shaker. Cobbler shakers are generally made up of a metal or glass tumbler, a tight-fitting metal lid equipped with holes for straining drinks, and a small cap designed to fit over the straining lid while the user is shaking drinks. They are made in any variety of styles from the simple to ones that are lavishly festooned with engravings and moldings. Sizes range from those large enough for multiple cocktails to shakers made for single servings. These shakers are marketed to home bartenders because of their user-friendly design. We've found that they often leak, however, and sometimes the parts bind together and are difficult to separate. As for the often ornately decorated pitcher or teapot shakers, it is best to leave these as display pieces for your bar. Designed for mixing multiple cocktails at once, they tend to be unusually large, and are awkward to handle.

So which shaker should you choose when setting up your first bar? Our advice is to start out with the Boston shaker, since it is a true cocktail workhorse. From there, it is always fun to pick up one or two other styles for occasional use. You never know when you'll stumble upon an antique shaker that will make for an eye-catching display in your bar or on your mantel.

HAWTHORNE STRAINER / This is the most popular cocktail strainer in the bartending world. Shaped like a miniature paddle with a wire coil around the underside of its perimeter, the strainer has either two or four flat "fingers" that are designed to attach to the metal tumbler of a Boston shaker. This tool is perfect for quickly straining any cocktail. It even fits snugly into the top of a mixing glass, which makes it well suited for straining stirred cocktails. If you're straining a cocktail with muddled ingredients, note that the strainer's coil has a tendency to pick up bits of muddled fruits and herbs, and it will need to be thoroughly washed before reusing.

LONG-HANDLED BAR SPOON / A long, spiral-handled bar spoon is an essential tool when working behind the bar. Its design is perfect for stirring drinks in a mixing glass, distributing ingredients evenly in muddled cocktails, and spooning sugar and other ingredients into glasses. It can even be used for layering spirits on top of one another. As mentioned earlier (see page 55), the spoon's spiraled handle is perfect for twisting the spoon while moving it up and down in a mixing glass in order to stir cocktails gently.

JIGGER / The jigger is an essential tool for measuring ingredients. We highly recommend it, at least until you've mastered the art of free pouring with speed pourers (we'll talk about those in a minute). Metal jiggers typically come with two cones, attached back to back. The larger one is actually the jigger measure and holds either 1½ or 2 ounces. The smaller one is the pony, and holds ¾ or 1 ounce. Typically, the smaller-size jigger comes with a smaller pony. We suggest that you have both the larger and smaller combinations. Fancier jiggers come with a handle. If you do not have a jigger on hand, a set of measuring spoons will do in a pinch; just remember that 2 tablespoons equal 1 ounce.

SPEED POURERS / Metal speed pourers are ideal for accurately free-pouring ingredients without the aid of a jigger or pony. Typically found in restaurant-supply stores, these spouts can now be found at many cookware stores that carry bar supplies. A speed pourer should fit snugly into the neck of your liquor bottles, making for fast, consistent pours every time.

When you first use a speed pourer, we recommend that you practice estimating your pour by filling an empty liquor bottle with water and pouring it into a measured receptacle, such as a jigger. Count the seconds from the moment liquid starts to come out at a steady pace until you have the desired amount of water. If it consistently takes you 3 seconds to fill a 1½-ounce jigger, then you know that every time you count 3 seconds while pouring, you've poured an accurate shot.

Remember to hold the bottle by the neck and keep your index finger wrapped around the base of the spout to ensure that the spout does not fall out of the bottle. If you're right-handed, when you start to pour, raise the bottle quickly to position, with the bottle angled toward the one o'clock position and the spout angled toward six o'clock. If you're pouring with your left hand, the bottle should be angled toward eleven o'clock, with the spout pointed straight down at six o'clock. When you've finished pouring, quickly rotate the bottle back to the upright position.

Free-pouring allows you to show a touch of style while you're mixing drinks. More importantly, it enables you to mix cocktails more intuitively. With enough practice, you'll be able to find balance in your cocktails simply by pouring what feels right.

JUICER / We've already stressed the importance of always using fresh citrus juices when mixing cocktails (see page 44). Now we'll focus on how to extract those juices. At the restaurant we go through juice quickly, so we squeeze it in large quantities with an electric juicer. At home, however, an electric juicer generally isn't necessary. If you're just going to be squeezing enough juice for one evening of cocktail mixing, there are other options from which to choose. The first, and probably most

time-consuming, is a citrus reamer. This is usually an inexpensive tool that can be pressed into the center of half a lemon, lime, orange, or grapefruit, releasing the fruit's juices. The main problems with this type of tool are that it doesn't yield a lot of juice, plus it creates excessive amounts of pulp and seeds, so you will have to strain the juice.

Better, but more expensive, alternatives are a countertop, lever-driven juice extractor and an electric rotating extractor. These do an exceptional job of squeezing every last drop from the citrus, though you still need to strain your juice. These extractors are perfect if you anticipate squeezing large amounts of juice.

Our favorite citrus squeezers, which are both inexpensive and especially well-suited for light everyday use, are the hand-held lime, lemon, and orange presses commonly found in Latin groceries. These little metal tools have a perforated receptacle that fits half of a fruit, and a handle with an inverted cup that is pulled down into the fruit, forcing juice through the little holes. There is no straining necessary with these presses, and you can simply pop the used fruit into the compost with a reverse snap of the two arms. If you have a supply of cut fruit prepped ahead of time, these presses are perfectly suited for professional use, and they are the only juicers that you should ever need when bartending at home. Regardless of you how you squeeze your citrus fruit, it's handy to know that a **MEDIUM ORANGE** yields about ⅓ **CUP OF JUICE;** a **MEDIUM LEMON,** about **3 TABLESPOONS OF JUICE;** and a **MEDIUM LIME,** about **2 TABLESPOONS.**

MUDDLER / A muddler is essentially a short pestle, usually wooden but sometimes plastic, that is shaped like a miniature baseball bat. It is used for mashing sugar cubes, fruit, herbs, and even ice in cocktails. Muddling, a technique that is most often used to make an **OLD-FASHIONED** or a Mojito, is an excellent way to extract flavor from fruits and herbs. By bruising the mint in a Mojito with a muddler, for example, the herb's oils are released into the glass, imbuing the cocktail with its refreshing essence.

Whenever you're muddling citrus fruits, such as the orange slice in an Old-Fashioned, it is important to mash the fruit enough to release the oils in the rind. This opens up a much fresher citrus flavor than simply mashing the pulp. Muddling is useful in bringing out the flavors of other fruits as well. Slice a strawberry or two, toss them, along with a touch of simple syrup, into the bottom of a mixing glass, muddle everything to a paste, and you've got the base for a great strawberry cocktail. Simply add ice, a touch of lime, and your choice of spirits, and shake and strain. You'll be amazed at the fresh, summery flavor that fills your glass.

Sometimes we'll add a few ice cubes to our mixing glass when breaking down fruits or vegetables for a drink. This allows us to break down the ingredients further and, at the same time, create some small ice chips that will remain floating on top of the drink after everything is shaken and strained. Generally, these drinks will have bits of the muddled ingredients floating on the surface of the drink as well. It all adds an interesting element of texture to the finished cocktail.

In truth there are almost no limits to what can be done with muddled cocktails. We know bartenders who reach for the muddler almost every time they come up with a new cocktail. If you don't have any way of extracting fresh juice, try

PEACHES & HERB

3 to 4 slices fresh peach, plus 1 slice for garnish

3 to 4 fresh sage leaves, plus 1 for garnish

Splash of Simple Syrup (optional, PAGE 116)

1½ ounces brandy

½ ounce Cointreau

2 dashes peach bitters

¼ ounce fresh lemon juice

——— MAKES 1 DRINK ———

In a mixing glass, muddle the peach slices with the sage and the syrup, if needed (depending on the sweetness of the peach), to make a pulp. Top with ice, add the brandy, Cointreau, bitters, and lemon juice, and shake until cold. Strain into a chilled cocktail glass and garnish with the remaining slice of peach and sage leaf.

JULEP STRAINER

PLASTIC SQUEEZE BOTTLES

OLD BITTERS BOTTLES

EMPTY LIQUOR BOTTLES

PITCHERS OR CARAFES

ICE SCOOP, BUCKET,
PICK, AND CRUSHER

CHEF'S KNIFE

MESH STRAINERS

POLISHING CLOTH

SMALL GRATER

MEASURING SPOONS

COCKTAIL NAPKINS, STRAWS,
SIP STICKS, AND STIRRERS

ELECTRIC BLENDER

CHAMPAGNE STOPPERS AND
VACUUM WINE STOPPERS
OR WINE GAS

muddling a wedge or two of lime in Cointreau the next time you're in the mood for a **COSMOPOLITAN;** we're willing to bet that you'll be pleased with the result. Let your imagination and muddler run wild; there's no telling what you'll dream up next.

CHANNEL KNIFE / At Absinthe we typically make our twists to order. To do this, we use a type of zester called a channel knife, which allows us to "unwrap" a thin twist of zest directly over each cocktail just before serving it to a guest. It is one of the little details that enables us to make even the simplest cocktail special. When we twist the zest directly from a fresh lemon, a burst of citrus oil covers the surface of the waiting cocktail; in that instant, a simple garnish becomes an integral part of the drink.

Although this tool takes a bit of practice to master, it's worth the effort. Your guests will be impressed each time you zest a twist for them directly over their drinks. The trick is to hold your lemon with one hand so that its length is parallel to the bar, and hold the channel knife with your other hand, so that the channel runs parallel to the fruit's equator. Next, twist the piece of fruit away from you while you pull the channel down into the rind and toward your body in one motion. Try to twist the fruit completely around so that the channel comes back to its starting point.

PARING KNIFE AND CUTTING BOARD / A good, sharp knife and at least a small cutting board are essential for cutting fresh fruits for garnishes, and for cutting ingredients like cucumbers or peaches down to size, so that they may be muddled into cocktails.

CORKSCREW, CHURCH KEY, AND CAN OPENER / You may not need all of these things at the same time, but a decent corkscrew and a can opener should be at your disposal. Being professional bartenders, we tend to prefer the "waiter's friend" style of corkscrew, whether we're behind the bar or at home. This is a compact, lightweight corkscrew equipped with a bottle opener, and can be easily tucked away in a back pocket when not in use. It also has a little blade for cutting the foil from a wine or spirit bottle, and also doubles as a box cutter for opening cases of liquor and wine. If you find the waiter's friend too difficult to use, no problem; choose any corkscrew that you like. As for a can opener, any household version will work; you just want to be able to open things like cans of pineapple or tomato juice, or a can of coconut milk, should the need arise.

TOOTHPICKS, MARTINI PICKS, SKEWERS / A supply of small picks that you can use to skewer olives, cherries, onions, and other garnishes will help keep your guests smiling, and their fingers dry. It can be a frustratingly wet and sometimes sticky task to fish that cherry from the depths of a cocktail without the aid of a cocktail pick. It really doesn't matter if these are the little plastic swords that your grandfather used to spear cherries in his **MANHATTANS,** or elaborately designed silver martini picks, complete with little olives molded to the ends. You're just looking for something to keep your garnishes accessible in the glass.

TOWELS / Professional bartending is wet work. We keep an ample supply of towels, some dampened to clean up sticky messes, and some dry to wipe up spills, condensation, and melted ice. At home it is good to have one of each.

GARNISHES

NO ONE WANTS TO BE HANDED A BEAUTIFUL COCKTAIL ONLY to notice that the wedge of lime clinging to the side of the glass is brown along the edges, or the lemon twist in the **MARTINI** is dried out and flavorless. Lemon and lime wedges, citrus wheels, and any other cut fruit should be prepared as close to serving time as possible. If you do prep them early, or if you cut extra fruit in anticipation of a big cocktail night, then keep the extras in a container in the refrigerator, covered with a damp paper towel. When it's time to set up your bar, you can use either bowls or small bucket-style glasses to hold the fruit, depending on the size of the space in which you're working.

Any time you use fresh herbs, whether in a cocktail or as a garnish, it is best to keep them on the stem as long as possible, since the leaves start to break down and lose integrity the moment they are picked off. To store your herbs, keep the stems immersed in a small glass of water in the refrigerator. If you don't plan on using much, then just take what you need from the refrigerator. If you require a large quantity, for example, enough mint for a Mojito party, then you can pick off the mint leaves in advance, cover them with a damp paper towel, and refrigerate them, just as you would pre-cut fruit. When it comes time to use the mint, take out only as much as you think you'll need for a short period, since the leaves will wilt quickly when kept at room temperature for any length of time.

We suggest that you follow tradition and always use an odd number when you're reaching for olives, onions, cherries, or berries for a garnish. One is the typical count for olives and maraschino cherries, but you'll often see three onions or small berries speared on a cocktail pick. It is considered poor form and a sign of disrespect to present a guest with two of any of these garnishes. Some bartenders may dismiss the custom as superstition, but we like to observe old cocktail rituals.

When you've come up with a new cocktail and you're trying to decide how to garnish it, think about the cocktail before you, and don't let yourself get caught up in convention. A garnish should either work as a component in the cocktail, such as a fresh twist that was zested directly over the drink, or it should play the role of an accessory to a cocktail, such as a celery stick that lends a savory crunch to a **BLOODY MARY**. A garnish can also work as a creative accent, such as the caramelized-sugar rim on our late-night cocktail, **THE BLACKOUT**. Think outside of the box; your garnishes can be creative extensions of your cocktails as well as of yourself.

MUJER VERDE

1 ounce Hendrick's gin
⅓ ounce fresh lime juice
¼ ounce Simple Syrup (PAGE 116)
½ ounce Green Chartreuse
¼ ounce Yellow Chartreuse
Lime twist for garnish

———— MAKES 1 DRINK ————

Combine all the liquid ingredients in an ice-filled cocktail shaker. Shake until cold, and then strain into a chilled cocktail glass. Garnish with the lime twist.

CREATED BY ABSINTHE BARTENDER, RAUL TAMAYO.

Here are some of the basic garnishes that you'll need for a typical cocktail party and suggestions for interesting ways to use them. When appropriate, we've also provided information on how to prep them.

CITRUS TWISTS / As we've noted earlier, twists are best freshly made, and we like to use a channel knife for this purpose (see page 72). The channel knife produces a very thin twist, which dries out quickly. So if you find it necessary to prep your twists early, it's best to cut wide strips of zest with a sharp paring knife. Start by cutting off an end from a firm lemon or a fresh, thick-skinned orange to create a base on which the fruit can be stabilized. Then, working from top to bottom, cut strips of zest from the fruit, following its contour. The goal is to cut long, wide strips up to 1½ inches long and ½ inch wide. You want a bit of the white pith to remain on the underside of the twist so that it will maintain its structure when it is handled, but not too much or your cocktail will taste bitter. A nice wide strip of zest cut in this manner will give a cocktail dramatic visual appeal and release a generous amount of citrus oil over the drink when twisted. Remember to rub the rim of the glass with the skin side of the zest after twisting. That way the citrus essence will be the first thing that greets your guest's lips.

FLAMED CITRUS ZEST / The wide strips are best for flaming citrus oils over a cocktail, which introduces a caramelized essence to the drink. To flame a zest, light a match and hold it in one hand. With your other hand pick up the zest by its sides. Hold it between your thumb and forefinger with the skin facing the drink, 3 to 4 inches above the glass. Be careful not to squeeze the zest too soon, or you'll release the oils before they are flamed. Move the lit match under the zest and squeeze your fingers together quickly, forcing the citrus oil through the flame, which will create a brilliant flash and land on the surface of the drink.

LEMON AND LIME WEDGES / Wedges are best when they are nice and wide. An average lemon should yield about 8 wedges and a lime about 6. To prepare lemon and lime wedges, start by cutting the fruit in half lengthwise, from end to end. Then cut an equal number of uniform wedges from each half. If you want to be able to slip your wedges over the sides of your glasses, after you halve the fruit, cut a thin line through the pulp of each half along the equator, being careful not to cut all the way through to the rind, before cutting your wedges.

ORANGE SLICES / Since oranges tend to be much larger in diameter than lemons or limes, they are typically sliced into half-moons, rather than wedges, for garnishes. To do this, start by cutting off the top and bottom from the orange, going just deep enough to barely reach the inner pulp. Then cut the orange in half lengthwise, from end to end. Next take your knife and, in the center of each half, make a thin cut through the pulp from one end of the orange to the other, being careful not to go too deep. (This will allow you to hang the garnish over the side of a glass.) Finally, place each half, cut side down, on a cutting board and cut crosswise into slices at least ¼ inch wide.

RUM CRUSTA

2 ounces Charbay vanilla rum

½ ounce Cointreau

¼ ounce maraschino liqueur

½ ounce fresh lemon juice

Extra-long lemon twist, preferably the zest of one lemon in one piece, for garnish

——— MAKES 1 DRINK ———

Combine all the liquid ingredients in an ice-filled cocktail shaker. Shake until cold, and then strain into a sugar-rimmed wineglass. Lay the twist in the wineglass, letting a bit hang over the side of the glass.

frankie's brandied cherries

6 pounds dark, sweet cherries

¾ cup sugar

1 cup water

¼ cup fresh lemon juice

2 cinnamon sticks

1¼ cups brandy

———— MAKES 8 PINTS ————

Wash and pit the cherries. Combine the sugar, water, lemon juice, and cinnamon in a large saucepan. Bring to a boil and reduce the heat to medium-low. Add the cherries and simmer for 5 minutes. Remove from the heat, remove the cinnamon sticks, and stir in the brandy.

Transfer the cherries to a jar and refrigerate for up to 2 weeks.

LEMON AND LIME WHEELS / Since they are smaller in diameter, lemons and limes can also be cut into complete rounds for decorative garnishes. To make citrus wheels, simply cut the ends from your fruit as you would when preparing your orange slices (see page 75), and then cut the fruit into ¼-inch wheels. If you want to decorate the side of a glass with a citrus wheel, just cut a slit through the rind to the center of the wheel.

OTHER FRESH FRUIT / When you're looking for other types of fruit to garnish a cocktail, choose fruit that is fresh and in season at your local market. Then think about the ingredients that are going into your cocktail and how they might complement the fruit you've chosen. Get creative with your fruit; you can introduce new flavors to a cocktail by roasting, grilling, pickling, or macerating it before you use it in a garnish. Peach slices lightly grilled over an apple-wood fire, for instance, might be interesting paired with a slightly smoky Scotch cocktail.

CHERRIES / Although they can be difficult to locate commercially, brandied cherries are relatively easy to make at home. They add a more complex sweetness than maraschinos and a rich, grown-up bite to your cocktails. That being said, there is something comforting and satisfying about pulling a maraschino cherry from your glass and biting into its bourbon-soaked core when you've finished a **MANHATTAN**.

OLIVES / When looking for olives to use in cocktails, you'll quickly discover that there are countless varieties from which to choose. As a general rule, Spanish-style green olives, without a pimiento stuffing, are your safest bet. At the restaurant, we use super colossal–size olives, with pits intact. You can offer a variety, however, such as garlic, blue cheese, or even jalapeño-stuffed olives. If you're feeling especially creative, try curing some gourmet olives in olive oil or even vermouth with your own blend of herbs, citrus zest, and spices. With any luck, you'll end up with olives that can double as a snack.

COCKTAIL ONIONS / These little pickled onions are a nice tangy garnish for hearty cocktails like a **BLOODY MARY**, and they are essential for a classic Gibson. There are both sweet and sour varieties on the market. We sometimes add our own flavor nuances by soaking them for several days in a strongly flavored spirit like Campari before using them as a savory garnish in cocktails such as the **NEGRONI**.

CELERY, CUCUMBER SPEARS, PICKLED VEGETABLES, CAPER BERRIES, AND OTHER SAVORY GARNISHES / Use your imagination here; there are countless directions in which you can take savory garnishes. Once again, choose garnishes that make sense for your cocktail, but that also represent your creative impulse. We've seen whole cooked shrimp and shucked oysters served with **BLOODY MARYS**, and pickled jalapeños floating in a spicy concoction of tequila, peppered vodka, and Tabasco sauce. In both cases, the garnishes were just outside the norm, but they were perfect for their respective cocktails.

SUPERFINE SUGAR / A glass rim coated with superfine sugar adds a bit of decoration and another layer of sweetness to a cocktail. It is an easy enough task, but it takes a

PLANTATION

4 to 6 fresh basil leaves

½ teaspoon sugar

1 ounce Plymouth gin

½ ounce Cointreau

½ ounce fresh lime juice

1 ounce fresh grapefruit juice

¼ slice grapefruit for garnish

——————— MAKES 1 DRINK ———————

Muddle the basil and sugar in the bottom of a mixing glass to make a paste. It should look like pesto. (You don't need to add any liquid here because there is water in the basil leaves.) Fill the glass with ice. Add the gin, Cointreau, lime juice, and grapefruit juice. Cover, shake until cold, and strain into a chilled cocktail glass, preferably through a fine-mesh sieve. Garnish with the slice of grapefruit.

NOTE: Add a bit of soda water and pour it over ice to turn this drink into a refreshing summer cooler.

bit of practice to get it perfect. First, put some superfine sugar on a plate. Next wipe the rim of the glass with a towel or napkin so that it's completely dry; a few unwanted drops of water can cause your beautiful rim of sugar to run down the side of the glass, creating a sticky mess. Once you've dried the glass, take a wedge of lemon or lime and run it around the outside perimeter of the glass so that you have a uniformly moist band around the rim about ¼ inch wide or less. Now hold the stem or the base of the glass so that the rim just touches the dish of sugar; your glass should be tilted at about a 45-degree angle. Spin the rim quickly through the sugar until the entire rim is coated with a fine granulated layer. Once the rim is coated, tap the side of the glass over your index finger in order to shake off any loose grains. Remember that only the outside of the rim should be coated. If you coat the inside of the glass, the sugar can end up in the drink and destroy the balance of your cocktail.

For an extra bit of excitement and an entirely different garnish, we sometimes coat a wineglass with superfine sugar and then pour in a bit of 151-proof rum. Next, we take a match or a lighter and carefully light the rum on fire. Once it's burning, we can hold the glass by the stem at a slight angle and slowly twirl it in order to caramelize the sugar around the rim. The longer you let the rum burn, the more you'll brown the sugar, creating a brûléed effect on the glass that is perfect for all sorts of warm after-dinner drinks. Warn your guests before serving them a drink with a caramelized rim, because the glass will remain hot for some time after the drink is served. Avoid using delicate wineglasses for this because it can be a bit of a chore to get the caramelized sugar off the glass during cleanup.

COARSE KOSHER SALT / Kosher salt is perfect as a garnish for **MARGARITAS** and any number of savory cocktails, such as those with a hint of tomato. Coat the outside rim of a glass with kosher salt just as you would with sugar (see page 76).

HERBS / Fresh herbs are a decorative and aromatic way to decorate your cocktails. When using herbs, think about combinations that make sense, such as garnishing a drink with a basil leaf if you've muddled basil into the drink.

NUTMEG, CINNAMON, CLOVES, AND OTHER SPICES / Nutmeg can be grated directly on a **RAMOS GIN FIZZ** or your favorite eggnog cocktail. You can also mix nutmeg, ground cinnamon, and cloves with superfine sugar and coat the rim of a glass (see page 76). We've even sprinkled ground cinnamon over a flame, creating a brilliant light show as the grains spark, ignite, and toast before settling on the surface of a cocktail. Whatever you decide to do with your spices, remember that freshly grated or ground is almost always the best choice.

WHIPPED CREAM / When we use whipped cream for cocktails, we don't beat it as long as we would if were spooning it over a dessert. It should be only slightly thick, not stiff, so that it can still be poured and will layer nicely on the top of the drinks. As you are whipping the cream, you can sweeten it with a little bit of powdered sugar, or you can introduce other flavors by adding splashes of spirits like kirsch or Grand Marnier, extracted flavoring agents like vanilla, or syrups.

PISCO SOUR

1 egg white
2 heaping tablespoons superfine sugar
1 ounce fresh lemon or lime juice
1¾ ounces pisco
Drop of Angostura bitters

——————— MAKES 1 DRINK ———————

In an ice-filled cocktail shaker, layer, in order, the egg white, sugar, lemon juice, and pisco. Shake vigorously for at least 30 seconds, so that the egg white becomes frothy and all the ingredients are well combined. Strain into a chilled champagne flute and top with the drop of Angostura bitters.

NOTE: Remember that you are using raw egg in this drink, so it is best to wash the cocktail shaker and strainer thoroughly between each cocktail.

CASTAWAY

3 to 4 chunks fresh mango
½ ounce agave syrup
1½ ounces Montecristo 12-year-old rum
½ ounce fresh lime juice
Small mint leaf for garnish

————— MAKES 1 DRINK —————

In the bottom of a mixing glass, muddle the mango
and the agave syrup into a pulplike consistency. Top
with ice and add the rum and lime juice. Cover, shake
until cold, and strain into a chilled cocktail glass.
Float the mint leaf on the surface.

NOTE: To make a punch (pictured left), turn the
mango into a purée using the same ratios of the
cocktail. Combine in a punch bowl and add a large
block of ice. Add ginger ale to bring a bit more life to
the party.

AGAVE ROSE

2 ounces tequila
½ ounce kirsch or another cherry brandy
¼ ounce fresh lime juice
¼ ounce Velvet Falernum
3 brandied cherries (PAGE 76) for garnish,
plus a splash of their juice

————— MAKES 1 DRINK —————

In an ice-filled cocktail shaker, combine the tequila,
kirsch, lime juice, and Falernum. Shake until cold, and
then strain into a chilled champagne glass. Sink a
little bit of the brandied cherry juice into the bottom
of the flute for color. Spear the brandied cherries
with a decorative pick and lay across the top of the
flute for garnish.

RAMOS GIN FIZZ

1 tablespoon powdered sugar
3 to 4 drops orange-flower water
¾ ounce fresh lime juice
1 ounce gin
1 egg white
1 ounce heavy cream or half-and-half
Crushed ice
Freshly grated nutmeg for garnish

———————— MAKES 1 DRINK ————————

Combine the liquid ingredients, in order, in a tall mixing glass. Add crushed ice—not too fine, as lumps are needed to froth the egg white and cream. Cover with a tall metal tumbler and shake. This is one drink that needs long, steady shaking, so keep at it until the mixture thickens or becomes "ropy," as some experienced bartenders like to say. When thoroughly shaken, strain the mixture into a tall glass for serving. Garnish with freshly grated nutmeg.

NOTE: Remember that you are using raw egg with this drink, so it is best to wash the cocktail shaker and strainer thoroughly between each cocktail.

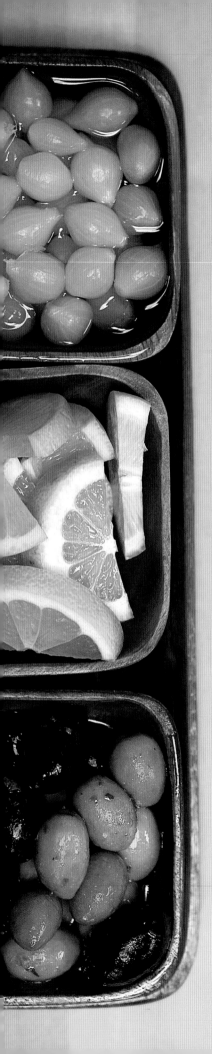

MISE EN PLACE

EVERY MORNING, AS WE GET READY FOR AN UPCOMING shift at the restaurant, we follow the same routine. We make sure our juices, syrups, spirits, ice, citrus wedges, and various other supplies are well stocked and ready to rock and roll. What we are doing is gathering our *mise en place,* which, roughly translated from the French, means we're putting our stuff in place. Although it may sound elementary, if we didn't follow this routine we'd probably find ourselves scrambling, in the middle of a rush, to cut the bucket of limes that we'd neglected in the morning. When making drinks at home, try to follow a similar regimen. If you take the time to set out as much as you can before you start mixing drinks for your party—ice, spirits, syrups, garnishes, sodas, juices, or whatever you think you might need—you'll find bartending is an easier task.

Similarly, when you are about to mix a single drink, gather your ingredients together first. At the restaurant, when an order comes in for a bold, smoky **OAXACAN,** we grab the mescal and Pimm's from the back bar before we begin (the Peychaud's bitters is always handy). By gathering our *"mise,"* we don't have to watch a perfectly good shot of mescal dilute over ice while we're scrambling to find a missing bottle of Pimm's. At home, when you're making your after-work **OLD PAL,** chill your cocktail glass while you pull the whiskey, vermouth, and Campari from the bar. That way, by the time you realize that you're out of whiskey and reach instead for a bottle of gin, switching your evening cocktail to a **NEGRONI,** your glass will be frostily awaiting the fruits of your preparation.

THE
100 PERCENT
COCKTAIL

2 ounces Swedish punch
½ ounce fresh lemon juice
½ ounce fresh orange juice
Drop of Angostura bitters for garnish

——— MAKES 1 DRINK ———

In an ice-filled cocktail shaker, combine the Swedish punch and juices. Shake until cold, and then strain into a chilled cocktail glass. Add the drop of Angostura bitters to the surface of the drink for garnish.

CAIPIRINHA

1 lime
2 tablespoons superfine sugar
2 ounces cachaça
Crushed ice
Lime wheel for garnish

——— MAKES 1 DRINK ———

Cut the lime in half crosswise, and then cut each half into quarters. In an old-fashioned glass or another medium-sized glass, muddle the lime pieces with the sugar to release the lime's juice and begin to dissolve the sugar. Add the cachaça and crushed ice and shake in the glass that will be used to serve the drink to combine all ingredients. This is one of the few cocktails that is served with the same ice with which it's been shaken. Garnish with the lime wheel.

NICKEL ROSE

1 to 2 dashes Campari
1½ ounces aquavit
¼ ounce fresh lime juice
¼ ounce fresh grapefruit juice
¼ ounce Velvet Falernum
2 to 3 dashes peach bitters
Orange twist for garnish

——— MAKES 1 DRINK ———

Rinse a chilled cocktail glass with the Campari. Combine the aquavit, juices, Falernum, and bitters in an ice-filled cocktail shaker. Shake until cold, and then strain into the cocktail glass. Garnish with the orange twist.

BUSTER BROWN

1½ ounces bourbon
½ ounce fresh lemon juice
Splash of Simple Syrup (PAGE 116)
2 dashes orange bitters
Lemon twist for garnish

——— MAKES 1 DRINK ———

Combine all the liquid ingredients in an ice-filled cocktail shaker. Shake until cold, and then strain into a chilled cocktail glass. Garnish with the lemon twist.

ELIXIR №. 1

¾ ounce Averna
¾ ounce Carpano Antica sweet vermouth
¾ ounce Campari
¾ ounce Velvet Falernum
Dash of orange bitters
1 piece orange zest with pith,
about 1½ inches long and ½ inch wide

——— MAKES 1 DRINK ———

Combine all the liquid ingredients in an ice-filled cocktail shaker. Stir gently for 20 to 30 seconds, until cold, and then strain into a chilled cocktail glass. Flame the orange zest over the drink (see page 75) and float it on top.

SENSATION

6 to 8 mint leaves
½ ounce maraschino liqueur
1½ ounces gin
⅔ ounce fresh lime juice

——— MAKES 1 DRINK ———

In a mixing glass, muddle the mint with a few ice cubes and the maraschino liqueur until the mint is broken to very small pieces. Add more ice and the gin and juice, and shake until cold. Strain into a sugar-rimmed cocktail glass (see page 76).

MONTE CARLO

2 ounces rye
¾ ounce Bénédictine
Dash of Angostura or Peychaud's bitters
Lemon twist for garnish

——— MAKES 1 DRINK ———

Combine all the liquid ingredients in an ice-filled cocktail shaker. Stir for 20 to 30 seconds until cold, and then strain into a chilled cocktail glass. Garnish with the lemon twist.

DEVIL'S PEARL

2 ounces Absente
¼ ounce anisette
¼ ounce Simple Syrup (PAGE 116)
1 to 2 dashes Angostura bitters
Splash of water
Lemon twist for garnish

——— MAKES 1 DRINK ———

Combine all the liquid ingredients in an ice-filled cocktail shaker. Shake until cold, and then strain into a chilled cocktail glass. Garnish with the lemon twist.

SHADES OF BEAUTY

WE'VE TALKED ABOUT THE STRONG IMPRESSION THAT a cocktail's appearance can have, even before the first sip is taken. We've also learned that shaking a cocktail can create a much different appearance than stirring the same drink (see page 55). But understanding and appreciating a cocktail's appearance goes deeper than just recognizing the difference between these two modes of cocktail preparation.

Two elements that directly affect a cocktail's visual appeal are color and texture. Color is more than just pink, blue, or clear; it can be the coppery elegance of a **MONTE CARLO,** or the mysterious pearlescence of the aptly named **DEVIL'S PEARL**. Texture is more than just the physical feel of a cocktail. Take the Monte Carlo, for instance: Its crystalline amber color suggests a silky feel, both to the eye and the palate. A **SENSATION,** on the other hand, with its green flecks of mint floating above the mossy depths of the liquid and surrounded by tiny grains of a sugared rim, suggests a heartier texture, both visually and physically.

When you set out to prepare a cocktail, think about how color and texture will play a role in the final outcome. Say you're shaking a **RAMOS GIN FIZZ**. You want to emulsify the ingredients to give the drink its pillowy texture, so you need to shake it longer and harder than you might a different cocktail. But when you're making a **RUM CRUSTA,** much of the cocktail's beauty is created by the dramatic allure of a sensuously long twist of lemon and a wide sugared rim, so extra care should be given to these garnishes. When you set out to create a new cocktail, you may need to experiment before you discover wherein its beauty lies.

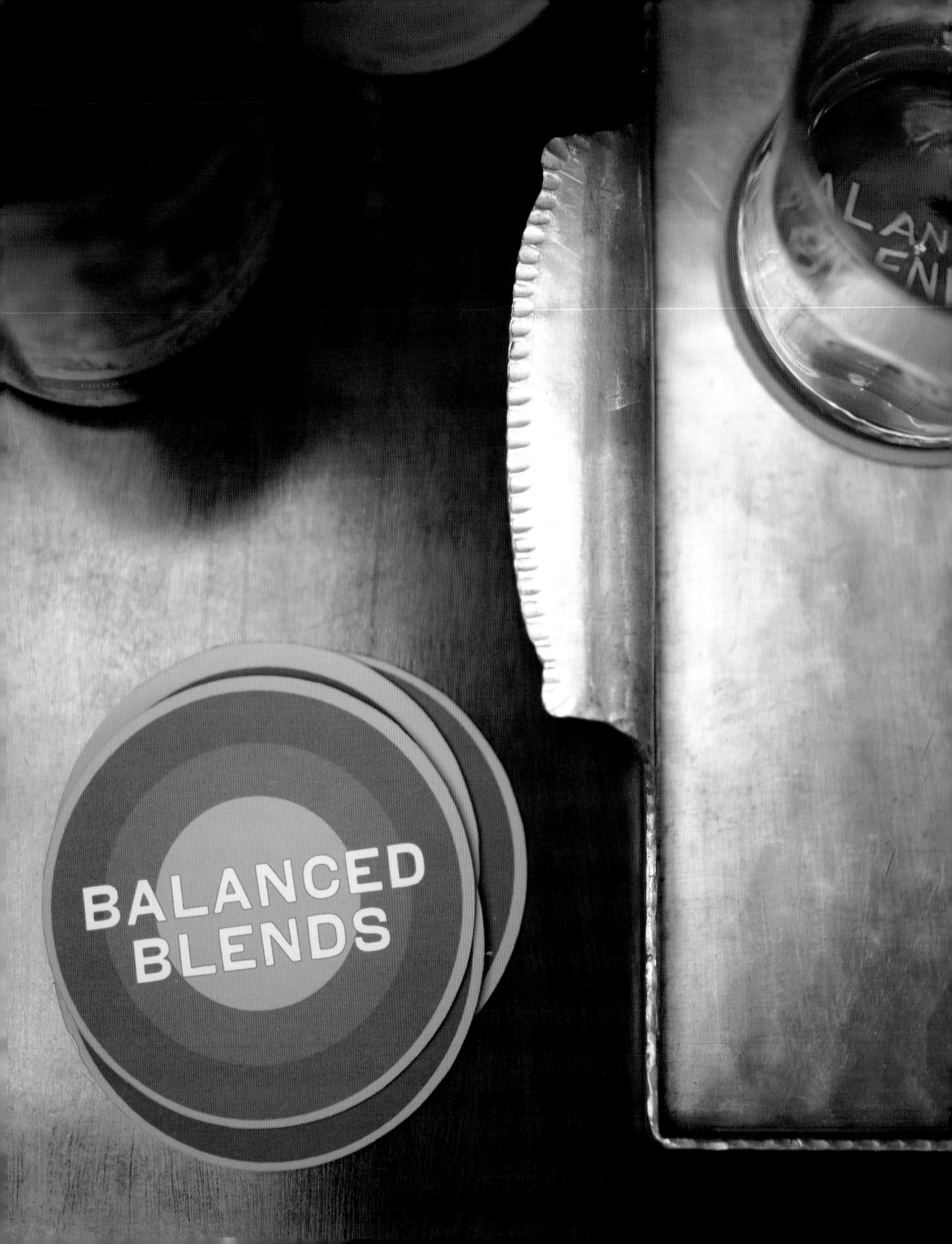
BALANCED
BLENDS

WHAT IS IT THAT MAKES A GREAT COCKTAIL—

THE QUALITY AND FRESHNESS OF THE INGREDIENTS

THAT YOU CHOOSE,

AN ARTFUL PRESENTATION,

OR

AN INVENTIVE RECIPE?

4

ALL OF THESE ELEMENTS PLAY A SIGNIFICANT ROLE IN CREATING a memorable cocktail, but there is something else that is essential, and that is balance. A skillful bartender understands that a good balance of ingredients and flavor profiles helps to make a cocktail superb rather than merely ordinary. Just as too much of one ingredient can ruin a dish, the same can happen with a cocktail. And there is nothing more pleasing than a drink that has the perfect balance of flavors and textures.

As epicurean bartenders, we treat our cocktails much the same as accomplished chefs treat the dishes leaving their kitchens. The chef knows that every component of a dish must work harmoniously with the others. It can be as simple as a salad of peppery arugula, freshly sliced sweet strawberries, and a bit of earthy Tallegio cheese. Gather a forkful of the arugula with a piece of strawberry, and the contrasting spicy and sweet notes dance together on your palate. Follow that bite immediately with a touch of cheese, and its pungent earthiness rounds out the dish. When building a cocktail, the goal is to use ingredients that similarly play off one another, and to find a harmonious balance among the components in the glass.

When you consult cocktail books, including this one, for new ideas, use the recipes as guidelines or even jumping-off points. In the end it is up to you, the bartender, to taste the ingredients you're using and work to balance them in the glass. For example, if you're making our **DAPPER APPLE,** you may decide to use Cointreau, a premium French triple-sec that is much drier than most other versions. In that case, you'll probably want to use more Cointreau or a dash more simple syrup to balance the acidity of the lime juice in the drink. That is, unless you or your guest prefers the cocktail on the drier, tangier side.

But balance isn't just a matter of countering tart with sweet. Let's say you're making **EL PRESIDENTE;** in our recipe we call for 2 ounces of Pampero Aniversario rum, which is dark with sweet and spicy underpinnings, and we mix it with ¾ ounce of Carpano Antica, a delicate, floral, and botanics-driven sweet vermouth. The Presidente is rounded out with a few dashes of Peychaud's bitters, which lend a dry depth. In our opinion, this cocktail represents the perfect balance among these ingredients. But if we were to change the rum featured in the cocktail to a drier variety with a bit more bite, we might be inclined to increase the amount of Carpano in order to soften the rum's edge and thus achieve balance in the glass.

Consider another drink, the classic cocktail **LA FLORIDITA DAIQUIRI,** a mixture of rum, lime juice, simple syrup, maraschino liqueur, and a splash of grapefruit juice. At first glance, this cocktail seems to be pretty straightforward. If you use a crisp silver rum as a base, you'll be starting with a light-bodied, refreshing spirit. The lime juice will lend backbone, and the simple syrup will soften its acidity. Used sparingly, the maraschino will add complex floral notes, but if you add too much, the spirit's intense sweetness will be overpowering. A splash of grapefruit juice, on the other hand, lends the slightest touch of dry, snappy bitterness, but any more than a splash and grapefruit is all that you'll taste in the glass. No matter which cocktail you are mixing, be aware of each ingredient's intended purpose, and work to help them all reach their potential by bringing them into balance with one another. Taste the drink each time another ingredient is added. That is how you will learn what each component adds to a drink and how they affect one another.

84 AND HAZY

1 fresh apricot, halved and pitted
¾ ounce white rum
¾ ounce aged rum
¾ ounce fresh lime juice
½ ounce Cointreau
¼ ounce orgeat syrup
¼ ounce mulberry syrup
1 mint sprig for garnish

——— MAKES 1 DRINK ———

Muddle the apricot in the bottom of a mixing glass. Top with ice, then add the white rum, aged rum, lime juice, Cointreau, orgeat, and mulberry syrup. Shake until cold, and strain into an ice-filled collins glass. Garnish with the mint sprig.

DAPPER APPLE

1½ ounces Citadelle apple vodka
½ ounce triple sec
½ ounce fresh lime juice
Dash of Simple Syrup (PAGE 116)
Lime wedge for garnish

——— MAKES 1 DRINK ———

Combine all the liquid ingredients in an ice-filled cocktail shaker. Shake until cold, and then strain into a chilled cocktail glass. Garnish with the lime wedge.

THE BEST TOOLS: YOUR SENSES

ONE OF THE FIRST LESSONS YOU LEARN AS A PROFESSIONAL bartender is to taste and smell everything all the time in order to understand how individual ingredients might play against and with one another in a cocktail. While tasting those ingredients is important, smelling them is, too, since it is usually easier to detect the subtle nuances of a spirit by smelling it than by tasting it. This is important to understand not only when trying to figure out which ingredients will work together but what their proportions should be. Sit down at Absinthe's bar on almost any night and you're likely to see one of us alternating between burying his nose in a glass and taking sips of the spirit that sits inside. It could be a brand-new product that we're inspecting, or something that we've tasted hundreds of times before. What we're doing is always the same—we're using our senses to understand, and ultimately ingrain in our minds, the flavor profiles of each of the ingredients that are the foundations of our trade.

Your home bar might not be stocked with the array of spirits that you'll find at a bar, but you can try sampling some when you are out for a drink. Sit down at your favorite cocktail haunt and, provided it's not too busy, engage your bartender in a conversation about different spirits. Perhaps they've got an extensive collection of American whiskies. Ask the bartender which ones are his or her favorites and why some are preferred over the other choices on the shelf. If possible, get the bartender to pour you a few tastes, or taste the whiskies along with you, so that you can discuss the different elements you find in the nose or on the palate of each one.

Or try ordering two **MANHATTANS** with a different bourbon in each one. You don't have to order both at the same time; just take note of how bourbon number one is represented before ordering the second cocktail. Ask your bartender to taste each drink as it's made, so that the two of you can have a discussion about the differences between the cocktails. If you find that you're particularly interested in one spirit, jot down some notes about it. The next time you drop by for a tasting session, you'll have a jumping-off point. Perhaps on another visit you'll want to try two Manhattan variations using the same bourbon, but with different types of sweet vermouth.

Once you've established a rapport with your bartender, you might be able to continue tasting spirits together on a regular basis. If your bartender is inquisitive like you, he'll see your tasting sessions as a way to enhance his understanding of various spirits and mixers.

Cocktail Detectives

JEFF / Behind the bar at Absinthe, we're forever tasting and challenging one another to identify the ingredients of new a cocktail. It can start by Rob handing me a drink he's been tinkering with and asking for my thoughts. Usually I'll give him an initial response about nuances that I find in the drink. I might like the way the aromatic spirit brings out more subtle elements in the cocktail, or, on the other hand, I may decide that it mutes the flavors of the base spirit. Either way, we'll usually start talking about ingredients, and he'll then challenge me to list everything that he's used in his new recipe. Determining whether the base spirit is gin, whiskey, rum, or something else is typically the first step, since that is easiest. The challenge gets more difficult when I try to pick out the individual producer, or specific bottling, of the base spirit. I may have figured out that he's using a Black Maple Hill whiskey, but is it the 16-year-old bourbon or the 18-year-old rye? Next I'll work on breaking down the rest of the cocktail, picking my way through the layers of flavor in the glass—aromatic or bitter spirits, muddled fruit or fruit juices, herbs, flavored syrups, or sweet liqueurs. As I do this I also taste for levels of intensity, or the proportion of each ingredient. This can be a difficult challenge, but it is completely satisfying to nail down a cocktail to its last ingredient. In the end, the challenges that Rob and I present to each other make us more educated bartenders and strengthen our palates.

NEW PAL

1 ounce rye

1 ounce Campari

1 ounce sweet vermouth

1 dash Peychaud's bitters

2 to 3 dashes pastis,
such as Herbsaint

1 piece orange zest with some pith,
about 1½ inches long and ½ inch wide

——— MAKES 1 DRINK ———

Combine all the liquid ingredients in an ice-filled cocktail shaker. Stir gently for 20 to 30 seconds, until cold, and then strain into a chilled cocktail glass. Flame the orange zest over the drink (see page 75) and float it on top.

OLD PAL

1 ounce Canadian whisky

1 ounce Campari

1 ounce dry vermouth

Orange twist for garnish

——— MAKES 1 DRINK ———

Combine all the liquid ingredients in an ice-filled cocktail shaker. Stir gently for 20 to 30 seconds, until cold, and then strain into a chilled cocktail glass. Garnish with the orange twist.

OUR RECIPE COMES FROM *THE SAVOY COCKTAIL BOOK* BY HARRY CRADDOCK, 1930.

VARIATIONS ON A THEME

WHEN EXPLAINING A NEW RECIPE TO PEOPLE, we'll often compare it to a cocktail they are familiar with made with similar ingredients. In the cocktail world, many drinks have a similar style. Take the **COSMOPOLITAN** and the **MARGARITA,** for example. Both drinks are made up of a base spirit (vodka in the Cosmo and tequila in the Margarita), triple sec, and lime juice. The Cosmo also has a splash of cranberry juice, but it does little more than provide a bit of color. Both of these drinks are known as sours. A sour usually includes a base spirit, a sweet element, water (in the form of ice), and citrus.

If you understand the basic concept behind a sour, you'll be able to make any number of cocktails in this style just by changing one or two ingredients. Replace the tequila in a Margarita with brandy, and substitute lemon juice for the lime, and you've essentially got a **SIDECAR.** Take away the cranberry juice from a Cosmo, switch from citron vodka to regular, and, if you're a purist, replace the fresh lime juice with Rose's sweetened lime juice and you've got Kamikaze. Or you could add a touch of simple syrup and keep the real lime for a fresher drink.

While sours are probably the most recognized cocktail category, drinks have been categorized by style since the early days of mixed drinks. Originally there were drinks such as punches, juleps, cobblers, and cocktails. A julep was made up of a base spirit, sugar (simple syrup), and some mint. Cobblers comprised either a base spirit or wine stirred with sugar, poured over crushed ice, and garnished with an abundance of seasonal fruit. Through the years, new classifications of cocktails have come and gone in an attempt to understand and document similarities between one drink and another. If you knew how to mix a whiskey cobbler, for example, you'd be able to mix a gin cobbler as well. Should you be truly interested in the idea of drink families, then pick up a copy of Gary Regan's *Joy of Mixology* (2003); he probably provides the most thorough treatment of the subject.

If you look at relationships among the ingredients of a cocktail, you'll begin to see how new drinks come together. Start thinking about ways to make slight changes to cocktails that are your old favorites. Make one or two changes at a time and choose new ingredients that can function like the originals—think sweet for sweet, tart for tart, bitter for bitter. Then taste each adaptation along the way, and eventually you'll find that you're balancing and mixing an entirely new cocktail that is essentially a variation on something you've already had tucked under your belt.

DEVELOPING BALANCE

WHEN WE DEVELOP A NEW COCKTAIL AND ARE THINKING OF combining ingredients that aren't typically used together, we'll start by inspecting each spirit separately. We'll pour a splash in a glass, hold it to our nose while breathing through our mouth, and let the aromas drift through our olfactory system. After a few gentle sniffs, we'll place a bit on the tongue by dipping a straw into the glass and capping the end with a finger, trapping a few drops of liquid in the end of the straw. We'll let the spirit spread over our taste buds and search for notes of sweet, salty, bitter, or sour as it opens on the palate. After considering how each element might show its character in the cocktail, we'll start blending tastes together in the glass to see if the ingredients will play harmoniously with one another.

The goal at first isn't to try and find exact measurements; we're simply making sure the flavors won't clash. If everything falls in line, then we'll move to the next step and start mixing test cocktails. It is rare that we come up with a cocktail that we deem perfect with the first shake. Even if we love the drink as it's first poured, we'll mix a few more, adjusting ingredient ratios each time in order to taste and compare one version with another. Many times, we'll have four or five glasses lined up next to each other, each filled with a slightly different variation of the same drink. As we taste our way through each of them, we gain a fuller understanding of how we want to balance our chosen ingredients. When we are doing this, we're always conscious of the fact that we're tasting alcoholic concoctions, so we only take small sips, and typically pass the rest off to our guests so that they may provide their input about the cocktails.

STRONG ENOUGH TO TIP THE SCALES

A COCKTAIL IS BUILT ON A FOUNDATION OF A high-octane spirit, which can range anywhere from 80 to 110 proof. Because of its high alcohol content, the spirit can be hot and not at all soothing on the palate when tasted alone. In many cases, a cocktail's firewater will make up 50 percent or more of its ingredient base. In order to create a drink that slides smoothly past the tongue, it is necessary to find ways to lower the proof of the core spirit. It's part of the art of mixing a cocktail.

Let's say you're going to stir up a **BOBBY BURNS** cocktail. Depending on the Scotch that you choose to feature, you'll be starting with a base ingredient that is in the neighborhood of 80 to 90 proof. That's pretty strong stuff. You can lower the alcoholic kick of the Scotch by introducing a healthy dose of a low-proof botanical sweet vermouth. (The ratio of Scotch to vermouth will vary, depending on the types of Scotch and vermouth you choose.) Stir these ingredients over ice, and the resulting chilly water will further dilute the mixture, leaving you with a soothing elixir that glides like silk over your palate.

In a properly made cocktail, the ingredients should work together beautifully in the glass, and the base ingredient should not overwhelm the others. Your friends may visit their favorite shot-and-beer joint because the bartenders have a heavy hand when pouring a gin and tonic, but mix them a **VENETIAN** with an oversized dose of 110 proof Old Raj gin, and they're likely to lose the notes of bitter orange, dry herbs, and rounded nuttiness contributed by the Campari, dry vermouth, and amaretto, respectively. In a perfectly balanced cocktail, the alcohol should be recognizable enough to be taken seriously when sipped, but it needn't be so intense that your guests are forced to down it over an unwilling palate.

A note about balance and its relation to the color of a cocktail: We saw in the previous chapter that color is a driving force behind the appearance of a cocktail, dramatically affecting how a drink is perceived (see page 85). The color of a cocktail can also be related to how well it is balanced visually. Imagine throwing an array of multicolored ingredients into a mixing glass and shaking away. Your final cocktail may taste sublime, but the color combination may result in a drink that looks more like a mud facial mask than anything your guests would want to sip. Is the problem the purple hue from Parfait Amour, an orangey liqueur, or the deep amber color of the bitter Italian aperitif Averna? Take time to think about the final color of your cocktails and how that color might be a prelude to the balanced blends your guests are about to enjoy.

BOBBY BURNS

2 ounces Scotch
1 ounce sweet vermouth
2 dashes Bénédictine
Lemon twist for garnish

—— MAKES 1 DRINK ——

Combine all the liquid ingredients in an ice-filled cocktail shaker. Stir for 20 to 30 seconds, until cold, and then strain into a chilled cocktail glass. Garnish with the lemon twist.

A POPULAR PRE-PROHIBITION COCKTAIL BORN AT THE WALDORF-ASTORIA, FROM *OLD WALDORF-ASTORIA BAR BOOK* BY ALBERT STEVENS CROCKETT, 1935.

SHERRY TWIST COCKTAIL Nº. 1

1 ounce sherry
½ ounce brandy
½ ounce French dry vermouth
¼ ounce Cointreau
¼ ounce fresh lemon juice
Pinch of ground cinnamon
Cinnamon stick for garnish

——— MAKES 1 DRINK ———

Combine all the ingredients but the cinnamon stick in an ice-filled cocktail shaker. Shake until cold, and then strain into a chilled cocktail glass. Garnish with the cinnamon stick.

CHOKE ARTIST

1 ounce Cynar
1 ounce Gran Centenario Anejo tequila
½ ounce fino sherry
5 dashes Regan's Orange Bitters No. 6
Extra-wide orange twist for garnish

—— MAKES 1 DRINK ——

Combine the Cynar, tequila, and sherry in an ice-filled mixing glass and stir. Add the bitters to a chilled snifter and roll around to coat the glass. Pour the Cynar and tequila mixture into the snifter. Garnish with the orange twist.

DUNLOP

1½ ounces aged rum
¾ ounce sherry
1 to 2 dashes orange bitters
Orange twist for garnish

—— MAKES 1 DRINK ——

Combine all the liquid ingredients in an ice-filled cocktail shaker. Stir for 20 to 30 seconds, until cold, and then strain into a chilled cocktail glass. Garnish with the orange twist.

TRILBY №. 2

1¾ ounces Scotch
½ ounce Italian sweet vermouth
½ ounce Marie Brizard Parfait Amour
2 dashes orange bitters
2 dashes Absente
Twist of orange for garnish

—— MAKES 1 DRINK ——

Pour the Scotch, vermouth, Parfait Amour, and orange bitters into an ice-filled cocktail shaker. Stir gently for 20 to 30 seconds, until cold. Rinse a chilled cocktail glass with the Absente and strain the cocktail into the glass. Garnish with the orange twist.

VENETIAN

1 ounce gin
½ ounce Campari
½ ounce dry vermouth
½ ounce amaretto
Lemon twist for garnish

—— MAKES 1 DRINK ——

Combine all the liquid ingredients in an ice-filled cocktail shaker. Stir gently for 20 to 30 seconds, until cold, and then strain into a chilled cocktail glass. Garnish with the lemon twist.

GRAND SLAM

1½ ounces Swedish punch

¾ ounce French dry vermouth

¼ ounce Italian sweet vermouth

1 piece orange zest with some pith,
about 1½ inches long and ½ inch wide

—— MAKES 1 DRINK ——

Combine all the liquid ingredients in an ice-filled cocktail shaker. Shake until cold, and then strain into a chilled cocktail glass. Flame the orange zest over the drink (see page 75) and float it on top.

QUARTERDECK

2 ounces rum

¾ ounce sherry

1 teaspoon fresh lime juice

1 dash Angostura bitters

Lemon twist for garnish

—— MAKES 1 DRINK ——

Combine all the liquid ingredients in an ice-filled cocktail shaker. Shake until cold, and then strain into a chilled cocktail glass. Garnish with the lemon twist.

EL PRESIDENTE

2 ounces Ron Pampero Aniversario rum

¾ ounce Carpano Antica sweet vermouth

3 dashes Peychaud's bitters

Orange twist for garnish

—— MAKES 1 DRINK ——

Combine all the liquid ingredients in an ice-filled cocktail shaker. Shake until cold, and then strain into a chilled cocktail glass. Garnish with the orange twist.

MISSISSIPPI MULE

1½ ounces gin

¾ ounce crème de cassis

¾ ounce fresh lemon juice

Lemon twist for garnish

—— MAKES 1 DRINK ——

Combine all the liquid ingredients in an ice-filled cocktail shaker. Shake until cold, and then strain into a chilled cocktail glass. Garnish with the lemon twist.

IS THIS DRINK SWEET?

ONE OF THE MOST COMMON QUESTIONS WE'RE ASKED at the bar is whether or not a cocktail is sweet. Usually someone will look at the list of ingredients, see some sort of simple syrup listed, and conclude that the drink is going to be a sugar bomb. Unfortunately, this assumption is probably a result of having one too many sugary sweet "candy-tails," which inexperienced bartenders try to pass off as properly mixed drinks.

A cocktail should never be overtly sweet, just as it shouldn't be too tart and acidic. You want a balance between the two, and that is what you aim for when pairing simple syrup, superfine sugar, or a sweet liqueur with an acidic or bitter element, such as citrus juice or a bitter spirit. The same is true when you're using an ingredient that has a heavy bite or is highly aromatic, such as Cynar, or Campari. You'll need to soften it with a touch of something that is roundly gentle.

You can achieve balance in a variety of ways. The sweet element can be a liqueur, cordial, or another fruit-based spirit, or even a fruit paste. If your cocktail needs an element of something sweet, experiment with some of these different options before you turn to the simple syrup; you just might find that you can combine the needed sweetness with an additional level of flavor.

To counter sharp or aromatic ingredients with softer flavors, take the same approach: experiment by pairing a variety of vermouth styles with a particularly florid gin when making your next **MARTINI**. Make one for yourself and another for a friend and taste them side by side to see how one ingredient reflects off the next. Consider using muddled fresh fruit together with freshly picked herbs to introduce new elements of rounded flavor and fragrance to your drinks.

SWEETENING AGENTS	SOURING AGENTS
simple syrup	lemon zest / juice
granulated sugar	lime zest / juice
fruit syrups	grapefruit zest / juice
fruit pastes	bitter spirits
cordials	—Angostura
sweet liqueurs	—Averna
honey	—Campari
	—Cynar
	—Fernet

MEASURED POURS

YOU'VE DECIDED ON THE COMBINATION OF FLAVORS that you're going to use in your cocktail and found the proportions that work best for your ingredients, balancing the sweet, tart, bold, and mellow flavors in your drink. Now how are you going to ensure that you can recreate the same results every time you mix the cocktail? The best way to do that is to measure your ingredients. You can use a jigger and measuring spoons to dole out ingredients, which will result in the most accurate replication of your drink. Or you can practice the technique of measuring ingredients with speed pourers, and then free-pour your way through your drink. If you're still mastering the art of free-pouring, however, you may find that you've poured too much or too little of various ingredients, and you may have to make adjustments.

There are a few tricks that you can use when you're learning to free-pour or you're experimenting with a new recipe. Start by pouring all of your ingredients into an empty mixing glass. We know that our recipes say to pour your ingredients directly over ice, but by pouring them into a glass first, you won't have to work quickly for fear of adding too much water to your drink from the melting ice. It will also help you eyeball your free-pour levels. The next trick is more of a money-saver than anything else: Always pour your least expensive ingredients first. That way, if you make a mistake and add too much simple syrup to your drink, or you accidentally drop an egg yolk in with the white for your **PISCO SOUR,** you don't have to throw out the base spirit.

What do you do if you've followed these directions and you realize just before you start shaking your cocktail that you've mistakenly added more lime juice than your cocktail will handle? Well, you could pour everything out and start over, but who wants to do that? Another option is to add a bit more of everything and rebalance the cocktail, leaving a significant amount of overpour in the shaker. Or, if you've got a friend around to enjoy the fruits of your mistake, add enough of everything so that you can make two cocktails. We don't generally recommend mixing two cocktails at the same time, but it's a better choice than pouring good ingredients down the drain. Finally, you could continue with the flawed cocktail in the name of education; chill it and strain it into a chilled glass, and then immediately make the same drink using the intended proportions. Taste the two drinks, one after the other, and see if you can identify the different flavor profiles and levels of intensities. While you may not want to drink the entire improperly measured creation, at least you'll have an opportunity to learn something from your mistake.

LA FLORIDITA DAIQUIRI

1½ ounces rum
½ ounce fresh lime juice
¼ ounce Simple Syrup (PAGE 116)
¼ ounce maraschino liqueur
Splash of fresh grapefruit juice
Lime wedge for garnish

———— MAKES 1 DRINK ————

Combine all the liquid ingredients in an ice-filled cocktail shaker. Shake until cold, and then strain into a chilled cocktail glass. Garnish with the lime wedge.

A CLASSIC HEMINGWAY-STYLE DAIQUIRI. OUR RECIPE IS ADAPTED FROM *TRADER VIC'S BARTENDER'S GUIDE* BY TRADER VIC, 1947.

BLOOD AND SAND

¾ ounce Scotch
¾ ounce sweet vermouth
¾ ounce cherry brandy
¾ ounce fresh orange juice
Slice of orange for garnish

———— MAKES 1 DRINK ————

Combine all the liquid ingredients in an ice-filled cocktail shaker. Shake until cold, and then strain into a chilled cocktail glass. Garnish with the orange slice.

Alternatively, fill a collins glass with ice, build the cocktail, and stir. Top with another splash of orange juice and garnish with the orange slice.

Rob and the 21 Hayes
(or The Invention of a New Cocktail)

ROB / One night, during my early days behind the bar at Absinthe, I was watching Owen Dunn (a bartender who has since left the restaurant to experience new adventures) as he stirred a **MARTINI** and garnished it with a cucumber. He was using a rose- and cucumber-infused gin that was new on the market at the time, and the garnish made perfect sense. My young cocktailian mind started to tick. I wanted to create a cocktail that would highlight the crisp, fresh, and subtle flavors of cucumber.

My biggest challenge was achieving balance in a cocktail based on such a light flavor. I started tinkering with different concoctions, adding nuances of flavor by playing with different combinations of syrups and liquors. I muddled the cucumber with various fruits, herbs, and just about anything I could get my hands on in the walk-in refrigerator. I even thought about asking the kitchen for an order of oysters so I could experiment with the brine. Then it came to me—Pimm's No. 1 is a cucumber's perfect partner. It is traditionally paired with cucumber in the classic highball the Pimm's Cup, a simple mixture of Pimm's and soda water or ginger ale. Pimm's is light enough so that it doesn't overwhelm the subtle crispness of fresh cucumber. In a small amount it would make for the perfect accent to a cucumber-driven cocktail. After that epiphany, finishing the cocktail was a piece of cake.

Pimm's No. 1 is a gin-based bottled cocktail, so gin would naturally be the base. The floral nature of the gin worked nicely with the cucumber, the same way mint and summer tomatoes work with cucumber in an Israeli salad. After mixing the ingredients together and tasting the results, I decided the only thing missing was a touch of acid, or sour (just like that cucumber salad) to bring everything together and round out the drink. I went with lemon juice because it's a natural with cucumber, it tends to be a bit drier than lime, and that is the direction I wanted to go with this cocktail. The 21 Hayes turned out to be the perfect cocktail to sip with a dozen oysters because of its light effervescence and savory cucumber notes. Of course a slice of cucumber was the perfect garnish, but to make it suitable for oysters in the afternoon, I reached for a childhood favorite, the underused cocktail onion, speared three to a skewer, and stuck it through the cucumber. Voilà! Now all the cocktail needed was a name, and "21 HAYES"—the San Francisco Muni bus line that chugs past our restaurant at least a couple of times each hour—seemed as good as any.

21 HAYES

2 slices cucumber,
plus 1 for garnish

¼ ounce Pimm's No. 1

1 ounce Plymouth gin

¼ ounce fresh lemon juice

Splash of Simple Syrup
(PAGE 116)

3 cocktail onions (optional)

——— MAKES 1 DRINK ———

Muddle 2 slices of the cucumber
and the Pimm's No. 1 in the bottom
of a mixing glass, breaking down
the cucumber almost completely.
Top with ice and the gin, lemon
juice, and simple syrup. Shake
until cold and strain into a chilled
cocktail glass. Garnish with the
remaining slice of cucumber or a
cocktail onion (if desired).

MUCH LIKE A
WELL TRAINED CHEF,
A GOOD BARTENDER
WILL LOOK FOR
INSPIRATION
ALL AROUND
WHEN CREATING
NEW COCKTAILS.

5

IN THE RESTAURANT IT CAN BE AS EASY AS RAIDING THE WALK-IN refrigerator to amass new ingredients, such as an unusual herb or an enticing piece of fruit. While you may not have the luxury of a fully stocked walk-in, you can find inspiration and new ingredients at well stocked supermarkets, ethnic grocers, and local farmers' markets.

Inspiration can also come from deep within the heart: Maybe you would like to recreate the essence of a special meal. One of our bartenders created a modern version of a cocktail he remembers his father enjoying years earlier in Mexico. At its purest, inspiration need be nothing more than the spark that ignites a desire to create cocktails that reflect your own spirit.

IRON BARTENDER

NEITHER OF US REMEMBERS EXACTLY WHEN THE TRADITION started, but at some point we fell into the practice of playing "iron bartender" on Saturday nights. Typically, a Saturday evening starts out as a mad dash toward a short finish line. Guests line up at the door between 5:00 and 5:30 p.m. dressed in their finest suits and gowns, ready to sit down to a celebratory pre-opera or -symphony dinner. **MARTINIS** are stirred, Champagne is poured, oysters are shucked, *coq au vin* is served, and by 7:30 everyone is on the way out, ready for the performance.

In the quiet time that occasionally lingers after the crowd is gone, we will steal a few moments for our ritual. One of us will present an ingredient—it can be anything, really, **a scoop of watermelon sorbet, rosewater, lavender, Dr. Schwartz's Bitters, egg whites, or a particular spirit**—say, a recently acquired gin. Sometimes guests who have watched us play the game before will ask if they can choose the featured ingredient; this is a challenge that we always love. Once it is chosen, just about anything goes.

Eager to earn the night's bragging rights, each of us starts pulling bottles from the back shelves and lining them across his end of the bar. Individual spirits are tasted, then combined with other spirits and tasted again, fruits are cut and muddled, and eventually the drinks start to appear. We won't let each other taste the newly created drink right away. Instead, we'll share it with the judges—the guests sitting in front of us. On a good night, Rob and I will each have a devoted assembly tasting and suggesting changes right along with us. At the end of the night, the only real prize is the ability to declare oneself a winner; but on the best evenings we both walk away with a few new cocktails in our repertoire.

ROB / A special trip, fond memory, or blessed event can be the inspiration for a new cocktail. I created THE LITTLE EASY to commemorate my wedding in New Orleans. To capture the essence of the New Orleans spirit my wife, Jessie, and I enjoyed as we celebrated our marriage, I designed a drink reminiscent of the SAZERAC. By following a traditional technique and incorporating new ingredients, I conjured up a new cocktail that is bound to stand the test of time. It is one that Jessie and I will surely sip together as we travel through the years.

SOURCES OF INSPIRATION

PUSHING EACH OTHER TO COME UP WITH NEW RECIPES under the pressure of a friendly challenge is definitely a fun way to craft cocktails. We also look to the world around us, our own obsessive hobbies, and the work of other bartenders and chefs for sources of inspiration. The fresh foods that we cook from the local market, the cookbooks we read like novels, and the culinary magazines that pile up in our homes all influence us when we're behind the bar.

While a cocktail book may seem like a more obvious source of inspiration, a cookbook can provide more stimulating ideas. We frequently use an interesting recipe as a jumping-off point for new drink. For example, the **SANGRE DE FRESA** was spawned by a dessert recipe. After seeing a recipe for thyme-scented grilled figs, we decided that nature intended that these flavors play with one another, and our **FIG THYME** cocktail was born. You could take the recipe a step further and grill your figs before muddling them, capturing another level of the recipe's essence. A recipe for an heirloom tomato–and-cucumber salad might inspire you to create a cocktail featuring muddled cucumbers and heirloom-tomato water. It may take a few tries to find a spirit or an acid (citrus or otherwise) pairing that you think works best with the flavors you've chosen, but once you have an idea of the taste you're after, you're halfway there.

A restaurant can also be a catalyst for the cocktailian mind. Whenever possible, we both love to go out to new establishments and taste the culinary tricks a creative chef might have under his toque. We sometimes encounter flavor combinations that we think would be successful in a drink.

We also use the Internet as a resource for new drink ideas. It's where we discuss cocktail theory, history, and techniques with bartenders and enthusiasts all over the world. We browse sites dedicated to the art of bartending, find articles about the history of a specific cocktail or spirit, or log onto discussion forums about the art of mixology. Some of our favorite sites offer new pros and home bartenders a chance to learn from masters of the trade, who provide their insights and advice and sometimes look for advice themselves. Connecting to a worldwide bartending community keeps us up to date on developing trends and introduces us to new recipes. We recommend a visit to Ardent Spirits (ardentspirits.com), the Internet Cocktail Database (cocktaildb.com), and Drinkboy Discussion Forum (groups.msn.com/drinkboy).

THE LITTLE EASY

Crushed ice

2 sugar cubes

2 to 3 dashes Regan's Orange Bitters No. 6

1¼ ounces single malt Scotch

¼ ounce Averna

2 to 3 dashes Herbsaint

1 piece orange zest with some pith, about 1½ inches long and ½ inch wide

——— MAKES 1 DRINK ———

Fill an old-fashioned glass with crushed ice and top with water.

Drop the sugar cubes into a second old-fashioned glass and add the Regan's orange bitters. Crush the sugar cubes with a muddler, top with ice, and add the Scotch and Averna. Give the mixture a gentle stir with the end of a mixing spoon.

Dump the ice out of the first glass and rinse with the Herbsaint. Strain the Scotch mixture into this glass. Flame the orange zest over the drink (see page 75) and float it on top.

INSPIRED BY ART

WE'VE ALREADY POINTED OUT THAT IT ISN'T necessary to use very expensive spirits in cocktails. There may be times, however, when you want to experience the intricate nuances that a super-premium spirit can lend to a cocktail. You may want to feature a one-of-a-kind drink for a particularly special occasion.

So when someone attempts to use a spirit with this level of craftsmanship in a cocktail, it usually is the inspiration for the drink. In such a cocktail, it is crucial that each ingredient highlight the characteristics of the spirit and not drown them.

Take our signature drink **THE CHARACTER**. Inspired by **GLENMORANGIE SINGLE MALT 10 YEAR,** a scotch with a range of subtle notes and flavors that is a sheer luxury of its own. We were eager to create something that could not just live up to the **Glenmorangie** name but emphasize the orange and tangerine flavors and hints of allspice. Once we moved behind the bar and began mixing, we created several concoctions that, like the handcrafted spirit, are like sipping velvet. Try it on one of your single malt–loving friends.

THE CHARACTER

2 ounces Glenmorangie
10-year-old Scotch

½ ounce Cocchi Aperitivo
Americano

Dash of Angostura bitters

Dash of sambuca

1 piece orange zest with some pith,
about 1½ inches long
and ½ inch wide,
stuck with a clove

——— MAKES 1 DRINK ———

In an ice-filled mixing glass, combine the Glenmorangie, Cocchi Americano, and bitters, and stir for 20 to 30 seconds, or until cold.

Rinse a brandy snifter with the sambuca and discard the excess. Strain the cocktail into the brandy snifter and flame the clove-spiked orange zest over the drink (see page 75). Drop the zest into the cocktail and serve.

COCKTAILS BY THE SEASON

OVER THE PAST TWENTY YEARS OR SO THERE'S BEEN a movement in this country toward using only very fresh seasonal and locally available ingredients when cooking. If you traveled back in time two centuries and told people about this movement, they would be puzzled, since that is how everyone ate in the past. Fast-traveling airplanes and automobiles had yet to come into the world, and large-scale commercial farming wasn't even on the horizon. Almost everything people ate and drank was made from local crops. Eventually technology and transportation evolved, making it possible to enjoy mass-produced foods from around the world any time of the year.

Today, whenever we use fresh ingredients in a cocktail, we try to follow the lead of this "new" season-driven movement. We muddle fresh tomatoes into a drink during late summer, and make the apple syrup for **JONNY'S APPLE SEED** during the fall and winter, when apples are in their prime. Using ingredients during their peak season encourages us to be inventive; one year we may be able to find out-of-this-world raspberries that just beg to be muddled in a cocktail, but the next year the berries might not be so juicy, and we'll look to a supply of ripe stone fruit for inspiration.

Keeping in tune with the seasons can also mean creating drinks that are appropriate for a particular time of year or an event that marks the season. Take springtime in the South, for example. No cocktail defines that time better than the Kentucky Derby favorite, the **MINT JULEP**. It's a refreshing thirst-quencher we associate as much with fair weather as with the Derby itself. Come the cold months of winter, however, and we're all more interested in a cocktail that warms the bones, like a **HOT TODDY**. The warmed brandy, perked up by a hint of cinnamon and anise and rounded by a bit of honey, is perfect for sipping on a chilly February evening in front of a fire.

We like to let the days and months inspire us when we're mixing new drinks. If it is a sunny afternoon in May, we may shake up a **LAVENDER SIDECAR,** its honey and lavender notes dance with the warmth of a spring day in the Napa wine country, where lavender grows wild. If it is cold and dreary outside, then a **PEARANHA** might be a better choice: The rum's sweetness paired with a crisp, dry pear brandy suggests the turning of fall leaves. Let the seasons be your inspirational guide when you're thinking about new cocktails; you'll find that each day presents new opportunities.

JONNY'S APPLE SEED

1½ ounces Calvados

½ ounce Apple Syrup
(PAGE 119)

¼ ounce fresh lemon juice

1 thin disk of a Granny Smith apple,
cut from the center

Sparkling rosé

———— MAKES 1 DRINK ————

Pour the Calvados, apple syrup, and lemon juice into an ice-filled cocktail shaker. Shake until cold, and then strain into a chilled cocktail glass. Float the apple slice on the drink and gently top with some sparkling rosé.

CREATED BY ABSINTHE BAR MANAGER, JONNY RAGLIN.

SOUR CHERRY BLOSSOM

1½ ounces Cognac

¾ ounce fresh lemon juice

¾ ounce sour cherry syrup

3 brandied cherries (PAGE 76) for garnish

———— MAKES 1 DRINK ————

Combine all the liquid ingredients in an ice-filled cocktail shaker. Shake until cold, and then strain into a chilled cocktail glass. Garnish with the brandied cherries.

ROSEBUD

Dash of rosewater

1½ ounces silver tequila

½ ounce Carpano Antica sweet vermouth

1 piece orange zest with some pith,
about 1½ inches long and ½ inch wide

Dash of Campari

———— MAKES 1 DRINK ————

Rinse a chilled cocktail glass with the rosewater, discarding the excess. Stir the tequila and Carpano in an ice-filled mixing glass and strain into the cocktail glass. Flame the orange zest over the drink (see page 75) and float it on top. Gently add a few drops of Campari to the surface.

TEQUILA GIMLET DE GRENADA

1½ ounces El Tesoro platinum tequila

½ ounce La Pinta pomegranate liqueur

½ ounce fresh lime juice

———— MAKES 1 DRINK ————

Combine all the ingredients in an ice-filled cocktail shaker. Shake until cold, and then strain into a sugar-rimmed cocktail glass (see page 76).

TOMATO KISS

3 to 4 'Sweet 100' tomatoes, halved

10 to 12 cilantro leaves

⅛ teaspoon kosher salt

1 slice habañero chile (optional)

1½ ounces silver tequila

¼ ounce Cointreau

¼ ounce fresh lime juice

———— MAKES 1 DRINK ————

In a mixing glass, muddle the tomatoes, cilantro, and salt into a paste. Top with ice and add the chile (if desired), tequila, Cointreau, and lime juice. Shake until cold and strain into a salt-rimmed cocktail glass (see page 79). For a "cleaner" presentation, this drink can be strained through a fine-mesh sieve.

GALAPAGOS

¼ piece Kaffir lime leaf

½ ounce Pepper Syrup
(PAGE 119)

½ ounce fresh lime juice

1½ ounces pisco

Splash of fresh grapefruit juice

3 brandied cherries (PAGE 76)
for garnish

⅛ ounce brandied cherry juice

——— MAKES 1 DRINK ———

In a mixing glass, muddle the Kaffir
lime in the pepper syrup until the
aroma of the leaf is released. Fill the
glass with ice and add the lime juice,
pisco, and splash of grapefruit juice.
Shake until cold. Place the brandied
cherries in the bottom of a chilled
cocktail glass and add the cherry
juice. Strain the cocktail over the
cherries and juice.

CREATED BY ABSINTHE BARTENDER, XAN DEVOSS.

THE WORLD IN A GLASS

A CENTURY AGO, BARS IN THE UNITED STATES and abroad served cocktails that were largely dictated by regionally available products. Take our old favorite, the **SAZERAC:** It was born in New Orleans because that's where Antoine Peychaud lived and sold his bitters. Brandy, which was originally the base spirit, was the most readily available spirit in New Orleans at the time. Lemon, which originated in Southeast Asia, found its way into food and drink in the United States because it was relatively easy to cultivate in temperate climates, hence the lemon twist. In fact, lemon juice and zest were common in many of the early mixed drinks and cocktails made in America.

Drinks that originated in other countries were born from popular and locally available ingredients. According to legend, in turn-of-the-century Cuba, a pair of American bartenders created the Daiquiri with ingredients that are synonymous with that country—rum, lime juice, and sugar. The **CAIPIRINHA,** on the other hand, is a Brazilian classic that could be viewed as a variation on the Daiquiri since it utilizes similar local ingredients, lime and sugar. But there is one notable difference—the cachaça, a Brazilian spirit made from whole sugar cane with spicy notes reminiscent of a silver tequila—takes the place of rum.

Before we had the options of a global culinary marketplace, bartenders frequently used the ingredients with which they were most familiar. In Italy cocktails like the **AMERICANO** were made with the Italian spirits Campari and sweet vermouth. Supposedly, the Italian bartender who first mixed an Americano wanted to mix an American-style drink, thus explaining the name of this quintessentially Italian cocktail. According to one explanation of the origins of **FRENCH 75,** a drink named after a World War II French artillery weapon, it was first made with Cognac and Champagne, rather than gin and Champagne as it is frequently made today. Although there is little evidence to support this theory, Cognac, like Champagne, is French, so it makes sense.

Today we can walk into a grocery store and find ingredients representative of just about every part of the world, while our best liquor stores are similarly stocked with an international assortment of spirits. If you want to create a selection of Asian-inspired cocktails for your next party, you will probably have no problems finding a plethora of suitable ingredients. Today there are few limitations in your way if you are an inquisitive bartender. Regardless of what you dream up, you'll probably be able to track down the ingredients.

Rob and the Tim Tam

ROB / After a weekend at a special bartending seminar in New York known as Cocktails in the Country, I returned home freshly inspired and ready to come up with some new cocktails. I started playing around with a few ingredients I had at home, dusting off some underused bottles, and cracking open the spirits I'd never gotten around to trying. But it must have been an off day, because my drinks were not coming together as smoothly as I would have liked. Needing to clear my head and reinvigorate myself with some fresh air, I left everything on the counter and went out for a walk. After all, you can only taste so many cocktails before you start to feel a little buzzed.

As I was walking around town, peering into storefront windows and glancing over the occasional menu at neighborhood restaurants, I decided to pick up something for dinner. I headed down the street to a local market that was well stocked with food from all over the world. Looking for something easy, I grabbed some hummus, baba ghanoush, and a few packs of naan and started to make my way toward the register.

About halfway down the aisle I stopped, almost dropping the pile of food in my arms. A line of dusty bottles tucked away on the top shelf had caught my eye. They were just what I'd been looking for—exotic syrups from around the world, such as rose, orange-honey, and pineapple. There must have been twenty different syrups on that shelf, which meant twenty interesting replacements for simple syrup. I was ecstatic. I put the groceries in my arms on the floor and pulled bottle after bottle from the shelf. It must have looked absurd; I heard a woman chuckling behind me as she walked past.

Pulling myself together, I settled on a single bottle of tamarind syrup. I remembered that I'd left a new bottle of 12-year-old rum sitting on my counter, and I thought the sweetness of this syrup would go perfectly with the rich, full-bodied rum. As soon as I got home, I pulled the tamarind syrup from my bag and started mixing. Within minutes I was sitting at my kitchen table nibbling on naan and hummus, and sipping on my new cocktail, the TIM TAM.

TIM TAM

1½ ounces Montecristo
12-year-old rum

½ ounce Citronage

¼ ounce tamarind syrup

¼ ounce agave syrup

1 ounce chilled black tea

Dash of Angostura bitters

Orange twist for garnish

———————— MAKES 1 DRINK ————————

Combine all the liquid ingredients in an ice-filled cocktail shaker. Shake until cold, and then strain into a chilled cocktail glass. Garnish with the orange twist.

SIMPLE SYRUP—A COCKTAIL STAPLE

SIMPLE SYRUP IS THE FOUNDATION FOR AN endless variety of flavored syrups that you can make at home. It is also a cocktail staple that bartenders often use, in its unadulterated state, to counterbalance the acidity in drinks made with lemon or lime juice. This syrup is nothing more than granulated sugar dissolved in water.

Like so many things in the world of cocktails, there are debates about the best way to make simple syrup. Some advocate mixing equal parts superfine sugar and cold water in a clean bottle and shaking the mixture until the sugar dissolves. Others think the sugar-to-water ratio should be increased to two or even three parts to one, and then the mixture should be heated over the stove until the water comes to a boil and the sugar dissolves. Our recipe falls somewhere in between these two techniques. Regardless of the ratios and preparation method you choose for your simple syrup, remember that more sugar means sweeter syrup, so when you are following a cocktail recipe you may have to adjust the amount of syrup.

Spiced Sugar

Get creative with your sugar. You can add or remove spices to suit the cocktail you're creating. Try adding a little cocoa powder to the sugar for a chocolaty note. Turn up the heat in your sugar by removing the cinnamon and other spices and replacing them with some cayenne pepper or chili flakes to use on the rim of a zippy summertime refresher.

---

simple syrup

1 cup sugar
1 cup water

——— MAKES ABOUT 1½ CUPS ———

Combine the sugar and water in a small saucepan and bring to a simmer. Continue simmering, stirring just until the sugar dissolves, 2 or 3 minutes. Remove from the heat and let cool to room temperature. Then transfer to a bottle that you can fit with a speed pourer. At the restaurant we like to use clean empty liquor bottles, but at home you might want to use something more decorative. Store your syrup in the refrigerator for up to 1 month.

spiced sugar

1 cup superfine sugar
1 tablespoon ground cinnamon
1 teaspoon ground nutmeg
½ teaspoon ground clove
¼ teaspoon ground allspice
(optional)

——— MAKES 1 CUP SUGAR ———

Stir together all ingredients in a bowl until well combined.

NOTE: Ingredient ratios can be adjusted to suit individual tastes.

SANGRE DE FRESA

2 strawberries,
hulled and quartered,
plus 1 small berry for garnish

4 to 5 basil leaves,
plus 1 for garnish

½ ounce Balsamic Syrup
(PAGE 119)

1½ ounces cachaça

¼ ounce Cointreau

¼ ounce fresh lime juice

Soda water

——— MAKES 1 DRINK ———

In a mixing glass, muddle the strawberries and basil with the balsamic syrup into a pulp. Top with ice and add the cachaça, Cointreau, and lime juice. Shake until cold, strain into an ice-filled pilsner or collins glass, and top with soda water. Garnish with the strawberry and basil leaf.

Ginger and Other Syrupy Delights

With a few minor additions, simple syrup can, be more than just a sweetening agent. Adding fresh herbs, sliced ginger, or whole pepper- corns to your syrup as it simmers on the stove will introduce flavors that can later enhance your cocktails. At the restaurant we make a ginger syrup that has become a staple; we reach for it almost as often as we reach for the plain stuff.

Making ginger syrup is about as easy as fixing your morning tea. We start by thinly slicing fresh ginger and adding it, along with a handful of fresh peppercorns for a touch of spice, to the pot with the water and sugar. You can add a bit more water to your pot if you want to simmer the syrup longer and extract more ginger flavor.

Just about anything can be steeped in simple syrup. We've become particularly fond of infusing herbs and spices in ours. We've used everything from thyme, mint, rosemary, lavender, to cinnamon, cloves, star anise. Be careful not to let your syrup come to a rolling boil when you're using fresh herbs; it can make them bitter. For subtle herbs, like thyme, you'll want to gently simmer your syrup for about 20 minutes if you want an intense thyme flavor, while a particularly strong herb, like rosemary, can simmer for 10 minutes or less. The same is true for spices: A little clove goes a long way, while star anise's subtle flavors need more time to show themselves.

You can also make different flavored syrups simply by using a different sweetening agent. Try mixing one part honey with two parts hot water and using that in place of simple syrup in your favorite bourbon or brandy cocktail. Go

lightly with a honey syrup to start; the flavor can be a bit cloying if used in excess. If the idea of honey syrup doesn't appeal to you, try making your simple syrup with raw sugar or turbinado sugar. Either will produce a syrup that is deeper in color and richer in flavor than conventional simple syrup.

Get creative with your syrups; they can add that extra element to your cocktails that will set them apart from the ordinary. Think about looking for interesting syrups at your local ethnic markets, too. Today any number of fruit syrups are available in specialty mar- kets, and they can be exotic additions to your cocktails. In fact, in the early days of the cock- tail, bartenders around the United States often used fruit syrups like raspberry, pineapple, and peach.

ginger syrup

2 ounces ginger, thinly sliced

1 cup sugar

1½ cup water

1½ teaspoons whole black peppercorns

––––––– MAKES ABOUT 1⅓ CUPS –––––––

Combine the ginger, sugar, water, and peppercorns in a medium saucepan over medium heat. Bring to a simmer, stirring until the sugar dissolves. Continue simmering for 30 to 40 minutes, or until the syrup smells very gingery. Remove from the heat and cool completely. Strain the syrup through a sieve, transfer to a bottle, and refrigerate for up to 2 weeks.

VARIATIONS:

thyme syrup: Add 5 to 6 sprigs of thyme (or more if you want a stronger flavor) to the sugar and water, omit the ginger and peppercorns, and simmer gently for 15 to 20 minutes. Cool, strain through a sieve, transfer to a bottle, and refrigerate for up to 2 weeks.

pepper syrup: Add 1½ more tablespoons of black peppercorns (or more for a stronger flavor) to the sugar and water for a total of 2 tablespoons of peppercorns, omit the ginger, and proceed with the recipe. Refrigerate for up to 1 month.

apple syrup: Add the skins and cores from 2 Rome Beauty or Red Rome apples to the sugar and water, omit the ginger and peppercorns, and simmer for about 30 minutes, or until the syrup has taken on the reddish color of the skins. Cool, strain through a sieve, transfer to a bottle, and refrigerate for up to 2 weeks.

lavender honey syrup

¼ cup dried lavender

½ cup honey

1 cup hot water (180° to 200°F)

––––––– MAKES ABOUT 1 CUP –––––––

Combine the lavender, honey, and hot water in a small bowl or the metal tumbler of a Boston shaker and stir to dissolve the honey. Allow the lavender to steep in the mixture until it cools, then strain it through a sieve to remove the lavender. Transfer the syrup to a bottle and refrigerate for up to 1 month.

balsamic syrup

1½ cups sugar

½ cup water

1½ cups balsamic vinegar

––––––– MAKES ABOUT 1¾ CUPS –––––––

In a tall, straight-sided, medium pot, combine the sugar and water and heat over medium-high heat, stirring until the sugar dissolves. Brush down the sides of the pot with a wet pastry brush to remove any lingering sugar. Continue to cook the sugar and water, gently swirling the pot occasionally to distribute the heat, until the water evaporates and the sugar caramelizes, taking on a deep amber color, and reaches a temperature of about 212°F.

Meanwhile, in a small saucepan, bring the balsamic vinegar to a simmer. When the caramel reaches the desired color, remove the pot from the heat and slowly add the balsamic vinegar. Take extra care when adding the vinegar, because it will bubble and pop violently when added to the caramelized sugar. Stir the mixture with a wooden spoon to dissolve any solidified caramel. Return the pot to the stove and cook over medium heat for about 5 minutes, until the mixture has thickened slightly.

Create an ice bath by filling a large bowl with ice water. Pour the syrup into a smaller bowl and then set it in the ice bath to cool, making sure the level of the melt-ing ice is well below the rim of the smaller bowl. Transfer the syrup to a small bottle with a lid and refrigerate. It will keep up to six months or longer.

caramel syrup

1 cup sugar

½ cup cold water

––––––– MAKES ABOUT ¾ CUP –––––––

Stir the sugar with ¼ cup of the water in a tall, straight-sided, medium pot over medium-high heat and continue stirring until the sugar dissolves. Brush down the sides of the pot with a wet pastry brush to remove any lingering sugar. Continue to cook the sugar and water per the instruction in Balsamic Syrup. Remove the pot from the heat and very slowly begin adding the remaining ¼ cup of cold water. Take extra care when adding the water because it will bubble and pop violently as it comes in contact with the hot sugar. Stir the mixture to dissolve any solidified cara-mel. If necessary, return the pot to the stove and simmer for 1 or 2 minutes to dissolve any hardened pieces of caramel. Once the syrup reaches the desired consistency, pour into a bowl and allow to cool. Transfer the cooled syrup to a small bottle and refrigerate. It keeps up to six months or longer.

LAVENDER SIDECAR

1½ ounces brandy

¼ ounce Cointreau

½ ounce Lavender Honey Syrup
(PAGE 119)

½ ounce fresh lemon juice

Dash of orange bitters

———— MAKES 1 DRINK ————

Combine all the ingredients in an
ice-filled cocktail shaker. Shake until
cold, and then strain into a sugar-
rimmed cocktail glass (see page 76).

Back-Porch Lemonade

ROB / This past summer a friend of mine invited me to his annual Fourth of July rooftop barbecue—probably because he knew I always end up at the bar mixing drinks for all of his bacchanalian friends. I thought about how these types of parties— most parties—work out. Usually you walk in and there on the countertop are bottles of booze, sodas, juice, ice, and my favorite—red or blue plastic cups. I always end up staffing the bar at this type of event because it's sad to see people slap together a pint glass with a ton of gin, a couple of ice cubes, warm tonic, and dirty lime. Most people want good, convenient drinks—so I figured out a way to premix cocktails with fresh ingredients, leaving me more time to enjoy the party.

First I scrounged up a few empty liquor bottles and, using some hot water and a knife, scraped off the labels. Then I filled them with quality ingredients using the right proportions to make my very own mix. Finally, to make it as dummy-proof as possible, I took a receipt, wrote the instructions on it with a marker, and taped it right on the front of a bottle. All the guests had to do now? Follow the easy instructions for quality cocktails, simple and spirited. They were a hit.

This is a really easy thing to put together whether you've got an invitation to a rooftop barbecue or you're having your own shindig.

back-porch premix

1¾ cup Ginger Syrup (page 119)
1¾ cup lemon juice
1¾ cup cranberry juice

———— MAKES ABOUT 1 ¾ CUPS ————

Use a funnel to fill an empty bottle with equal parts Ginger Syrup (page 119) and freshly squeezed lemon juice. Then add cranberry juice until you get a nice shade of pink. Toss the cap on, give it a shake, and you're done. Keep refrigerated until ready to use; it will last for a couple of days.

BACK-PORCH LEMONADE

2 ounces Back-Porch Premix (above)
2 ounces citron vodka
Ginger ale to fill
Lemon wedge for garnish

———— MAKES 1 DRINK ————

Fill a glass with ice and add 1 part mix and 1 part vodka (citron works nicely, but it is not imperative). Top with ginger ale and stir. You can make this stronger or weaker, or transform it into a very tasty virgin cocktail. Just omit the vodka and stir 1 part mix with 2 parts ginger ale. Garnish with the lemon wedge.

THIS RECIPE IS ADAPTED FROM CITRON LEMONADE.

FIG THYME

(pictured left)

1 fig, quartered,
plus 1 extra quarter for garnish
½ ounce Thyme Syrup (page 119)
½ ounce fresh lime juice
1½ ounces pisco
¼ ounce Cointreau
Sprig of thyme for garnish

———— MAKES 1 DRINK ————

In a mixing glass, muddle the quartered fig with the thyme syrup. Top with ice and add the lime juice, pisco, and Cointreau. Shake until cold, and then strain through a fine-mesh sieve into a chilled cocktail glass. Garnish with the remaining quarter of fig and a sprig of thyme.

DAEDALUS

2 ounces Irish whiskey
½ ounce Ginger Syrup (PAGE 119)
Dash of orange bitters
Orange twist for garnish

———— MAKES 1 DRINK ————

Combine all the liquid ingredients in an ice-filled cocktail shaker. Stir gently for 20 to 30 seconds, until cold, and then strain into a chilled cocktail glass. Garnish with the orange twist.

CREATED BY FORMER ABSINTHE BAR MANAGER, OWEN DUNN.

31 FLAVORS

¾ ounce gin
¼ ounce Pimm's No. 1
¼ ounce Velvet Falernum
¼ ounce Cointreau
¼ ounce fresh grapefruit juice
¼ ounce cranberry juice
¼ ounce fresh lemon juice
Dash of orange bitters
Dash of peach bitters
Lemon twist for garnish
Lime twist for garnish

———— MAKES 1 DRINK ————

Combine all the liquid ingredients in an ice-filled cocktail shaker. Shake until cold, and then strain into a chilled cocktail glass. Garnish with the lemon and lime twists wrapped around each other like a DNA strand.

PERGRONI

1 ounce Italian sweet vermouth
1 ounce Campari
1 ounce Pernod
Dash of orange bitters
Orange twist for garnish

———— MAKES 1 DRINK ————

Combine all the liquid ingredients in an ice-filled cocktail shaker. Stir gently for 20 to 30 seconds, until cold, and then strain into a chilled cocktail glass. Garnish with the orange twist.

PEARANHA

1 ounce spiced rum

¾ ounce Clear Creek pear brandy

¼ ounce Ginger Syrup (PAGE 119)

¼ ounce fresh lime juice

¼ ounce fresh orange juice

1 piece crystallized ginger (optional)

———— MAKES 1 DRINK ————

Combine all the liquid ingredients in an ice-filled cocktail shaker. Shake until cold, and then strain into a chilled cocktail glass. Press the crystallized ginger onto the rim of the glass if you wish.

MULBERRY STREET SLING

2 ounces gin

1 ounce fresh lemon juice

½ ounce mulberry syrup

Soda water

Fresh seasonal berries for garnish (optional)

———— MAKES 1 DRINK ————

Combine the gin, lemon juice, and mulberry syrup in an ice-filled cocktail shaker and shake until cold. Strain into an ice-filled collins glass, and top with soda. Float berries on the surface for garnish if you wish.

BOB-TAILED NAG

2 ounces Michter's single-barrel
straight rye whiskey

½ ounce Cocchi Barolo Chinato

3 dashes mint bitters

Lemon twist for garnish

———— MAKES 1 DRINK ————

Combine all the liquid ingredients in
an ice-filled cocktail shaker. Stir
gently for 20 to 30 seconds, until
cold, and then strain into a chilled
cocktail glass. Garnish with the lemon
twist.

CREATED BY ABSINTHE BAR MANAGER, JONNY RAGLIN.

IT'S THE END OF THE EVENING.

DINNER WENT OFF WITHOUT A HITCH.

EVERYBODY LOVED THE WINE SELECTION.

YOUR GUESTS ARE SITTING IN YOUR CANDLELIT LIVING ROOM
CHATTING ABOUT HOW THEY'VE HAD A LOVELY TIME.

SEIZE THE MOMENT

TO OFFER ONE MORE INDULGENCE:

AN AFTER-DINNER COCKTAIL.

6

LATE-NIGHT COCKTAILS ARE A SPECIAL TREAT, AND THEY SHOULD be approached with the same care that you use when preparing any favorite cocktail. Balance, color, presentation, and your own inspiration should all play a part in the cocktail you serve. Remember, it's late, so you won't want to overwhelm your guests with something large and too boozy. Choose a small port glass to serve an **ELIXIR NO. 2;** your guests will savor the way it soothes the spirit after a satisfying meal. Or reach for a single-malt Scotch glass for your **OAXACAN,** and show off the smoky digestif nature of the cocktail.

If you're going to forgo dessert at a dinner party, you might want to select a cocktail that satisfies your guests' sweet tooth, like the **CANDIED APPLE.** Let your intuition be your guide. You've already shown your guests that you're an artful host, so trust that they'll eagerly share that one last cocktail experience you have to offer.

The Blackout

JEFF / DECEMBER 20, 2003, STARTED OUT at Absinthe like any other night. Hungry and thirsty guests ducked in from the cold San Francisco rain, eager to sit down to dinner before heading off to see the *Nutcracker,* or to join friends at the bar for a relaxing cocktail after a long day of shopping. After all, this was the last Saturday before Christmas. We were settling into our night as well; these preholiday nights were always guaranteed to keep us moving through an impromptu choreography, otherwise known as bartending. The dance had only just begun to catch momentum when the lights were cut.

Somewhere between 6 or 7 P.M. the restaurant lost all power and went completely dark. Despite being buried knee-deep in the weeds, trying to knock out drinks for a fully packed restaurant and serving cocktails and food to a bar crowded with people, the moment the darkness hit, everything stopped. Unsure of how long the outage would last, the hosts stopped seating newly arriving guests in the dining room, but the decision was made to keep the bar open for as long as possible. If you've ever had the privilege of being in a bar when the power goes out, then you know it can be quite a festive occasion. The glow of the candles and the jovial warmth in the air give the illusion that you're a part of something special, an almost secret experience that no one but those seated at the bar will understand. It is almost like gathering around an indoor campfire, yet rather than roasting marshmallows, there is a full bar and ably equipped bartenders providing libationary treats.

At some point during the blackout Rob decided he wanted to have his own "candle," so he poured a bit of Lemon Heart 151 Demerara rum onto a small plate and lit it on fire. The alcohol burned in a wide blue flame, and sparked me to try something. Watching Rob's blue candle burn on the bar, we decided to sugar the rim of a martini glass and try to caramelize sugar directly onto the rim using the 151's flame. The glass had to be held over the flame at an angle while the melting sugar dripped down the sides of the glass, making quite a mess. We pulled out another plate, placed two sugar cubes on it, poured out another shot of 151 and lit the whole thing on fire. This time the sugar, saturated with rum, burned and caramelized right there on the plate. As if Rob's first plate of fire hadn't drawn enough attention to the bar, now all eyes in the house were fixated our way. Being behind the bar always has a stage-like effect, but this time we'd created an entirely new spotlight.

We proceeded to combine, shake, and strain the base ingredients into a martini glass, topping the concoction off with a layer of whipped cream. By this time, the sugar on the plate had melted into an acceptable caramel, and using a napkin, Rob picked up the hot plate and drizzled the warm caramel over the top of the whipped cream. Our pyrotechnic creation was complete, and everyone at the bar was eager for a taste. We slid the drink across the bar to a guest. He picked up the glass, paused for a moment to admire the drink before him, and then took a sip. With a smile and a nod of approval, he passed the drink to the guest seated next to him. Many more of the same were poured that evening, giving birth to the cocktail that would eventually evolve into THE BLACKOUT.

THE BLACKOUT

Spiced Sugar for rimming glass
(PAGE 116)

½ ounce 151 proof rum

3 ounces hot Leaves de Provence tea
or another floral tea

¾ ounce amaretto

¾ ounce Grand Marnier

½ ounce white crème de cacao

Lightly whipped and
sweetened heavy cream

 MAKES 1 DRINK

Coat the rim of a thick wineglass with the
sugar (see page 76) and add the rum.
Using a lighter, ignite the rum. Twirl the
glass to caramelize the sugar, making
sure you keep the glass upright, so
that no burning liquid reaches the
floor. When the sugar is caramelized,
put the fire out by pouring tea into
the glass, and add the amaretto,
Grand Marnier, and crème de cacao.
Top with the whipped cream.

LEMON MERINGUE

Juice of ½ lemon
1½ ounces Hangar 1 Buddha's Hand citron vodka
½ ounce Simple Syrup (PAGE 116)
½ ounce Sylk Cream liqueur
Candied lemon peel for garnish

—————— MAKES 1 DRINK ——————

Combine all the liquid ingredients in an ice-filled cocktail shaker. Shake until cold, and then strain into a chilled cocktail glass. Lay the lemon peel over the cocktail for garnish.

CANDIED APPLE

Spiced Sugar for rimming glass (PAGE 116)
2 ounces Calvados
¾ ounce Caramel Syrup (PAGE 119)
¼ ounce Berentzen Apfel Korn liqueur

—————— MAKES 1 DRINK ——————

Coat the rim of a cocktail glass with the spiced sugar (see page 76). Pour the Calvados, syrup, and Apfel Korn into an ice-filled cocktail shaker. Shake until cold, and then strain into the cocktail glass.

OAXACAN

2 ounces Talapa mescal
1 ounce Pimm's No. 1
3 dashes Peychaud's bitters
Orange twist for garnish

—————— MAKES 1 DRINK ——————

Combine all the liquid ingredients in an ice-filled cocktail shaker. Stir gently for 20 to 30 seconds, until cold, and then strain into a chilled cocktail glass. Garnish with the orange twist.

SPANISH COFFEE

1 ounce 151 proof rum
Ground cinnamon
½ cup hot coffee
½ ounce Kahlúa
Lightly whipped and sweetened heavy cream

—————— MAKES 1 DRINK ——————

Coat the rim of a thick wineglass with the sugar (see page 76) and add the rum. Using a lighter, ignite the rum. Twirl the glass and sprinkle the fire with the cinnamon. Be careful, this will generate some large bursts of fire! And make sure you keep the glass upright, so that no burning liquid reaches the floor. When the sugar is caramelized around the rim of the glass, put out the fire by pouring coffee into the glass. Add the Kahlúa and top with whipped cream.

KEY LIME PIE

2 Key limes, halved

½ ounce Simple Syrup
(PAGE 116)

1½ ounces Charbay Key Lime vodka

¼ ounce Sylk Cream liqueur

Liquor 43, or another
vanilla-flavored liquor

Crumbled almond biscotti for garnish

——— MAKES 1 DRINK ———

In a mixing glass, muddle the Key limes with the simple syrup to release their juice. Fill with ice and add the vodka and cream liqueur. Shake until cold. Rinse a chilled cocktail glass with the Liquor 43 and strain the cocktail into the glass. Sprinkle the biscotti over the top of the drink.

BLACK BOMBER

1 shot espresso

¼ ounce anisette

1½ ounces light gin,
preferably Baffert's

Dash of orange bitters (optional)

3 espresso beans for garnish

—————— MAKES 1 DRINK ——————

Pour the espresso into an empty
mixing glass and add the anisette,
gin, and bitters, if using. Fill with ice,
shake until cold, and then strain into
a chilled cocktail glass. The drink will
be foamy; float the espresso beans
on top of the foam.

THE COCKTAIL AS A DIGESTIF

A WELL CONCEIVED LATE-NIGHT COCKTAIL CAN SERVE the same purpose as a digestif after a large meal. Digestifs are typically aromatic, herbal, and often bitter spirits that can help you digest your dinner. Fernet Branca is an Italian-style bitters that is frequently used for that purpose. It also happens to be many bartenders' favorite after-work sipper. The herbal nature and bitter qualities of a digestif help cleanse the palate and get the digestive tract working.

Some spirits are sipped after dinner like a digestif, including Calvados or other brandy, aged tequila, single-malt Scotch, sherry, and many eau-de-vies, which are clear, fruit-based spirits (the translation from the French is literally "water of life"). While these spirits may not have the bitter and herbal qualities of a true digestif, they are distinctive enough to stand up and be noticed after a complex meal, and they definitely wake up the palate at the end of the night.

When we're dreaming up after-dinner cocktails, we frequently like to mix something that is reminiscent of a digestif. The **ELIXIR NO. 2** cocktail, mentioned earlier, is a perfect example of a digestif cocktail. The herbal qualities of the gin combine with the minty and refreshing elements of the crème de menthe, opening up the palate and soothing the stomach. Other cocktails, such as the **BLACK BOMBER,** serve a double purpose. In lieu of a digestif, many people like to sip a cup of coffee or a shot of espresso after a meal. Well, the Black Bomber offers the best of both worlds: The shot of espresso combined with a bit of anisette and a shot of gin provide a coffee fix and the digestif qualities of anisette.

To recreate the essence of a pure digestif, you can mix a traditional one, such as Fernet Branca, into your cocktail. Just keep in mind that a little goes a long way. The herbaceous, bitter, and aromatic qualities of the digestif should merely accent your cocktail, and the remaining ingredients should enhance that accent. A well-made digestif cocktail should be dry, slightly herbal or even smoky, stunning in appearance, and friendly to the palate all at the same time. Try experimenting with your favorite after-dinner spirit and let it guide you toward creating your own digestif cocktail.

We love to plan an after-hours party with our friends so that we can discuss a baseball game, a play, or even a meal. At home we like to offer coffee and tea, both decaf and regular; a selection of desserts or cheeses waiting at room temperature; and a few eyebrow-raising after-dinner cocktails to delight the senses and add one last parting gift.

INTOSATO NOCE

1½ ounces Plymouth gin

⅓ ounce Oloroso sherry

⅓ ounce Cynar

2 dashes orange bitters

Orange twist for garnish

——— MAKES 1 DRINK ———

Combine all the liquid ingredients in an ice-filled cocktail shaker. Stir gently for 20 to 30 seconds, until cold, and then strain into a chilled cocktail glass. Garnish with the orange twist.

ELIXIR N⁰. 2

1½ ounces gin

½ ounce white crème de menthe

½ ounce maraschino liqueur

½ ounce brandy

Lemon twist for garnish

——— MAKES 1 DRINK ———

Combine all the liquid ingredients in an ice-filled cocktail shaker. Stir for 20 to 30 seconds, until cold, and then strain into a chilled cocktail glass. Garnish with the lemon twist.

RECIPE ADAPTED FROM *BURKE'S COMPLETE COCKTAIL & DRINKING RECIPES* BY HARMAN BURNEY BURKE, 1934.

BORED STIFF

Extra-long lemon twist,
preferably the zest of 1 lemon
in one piece, for garnish (see PAGE 75)

1 ounce tawny port

½ ounce amaretto

½ ounce white crème de cacao

Dash of orange bitters

——— MAKES 1 DRINK ———

Put the twist in a chilled champagne flute so that it coils around the inside of the glass. Pour the liquid ingredients into an ice-filled cocktail shaker. Stir gently for 20 to 30 seconds, until cold, and then strain into the flute.

LAST CALL

1½ ounces Calvados

¾ ounce Tuaca

Dash of orange bitters

1 piece orange zest with some pith,
about 1½ inches long and ½ inch wide

——— MAKES 1 DRINK ———

Combine all the liquid ingredients in an ice-filled cocktail shaker. Stir for 20 to 30 seconds until cold, and then strain into a chilled rocks glass. Flame the orange zest over the drink (see page 75) and float it on top.

DEVIL'S OWN

½ to ¾ ounce orange brandy,
preferably Prime Arance

½ cup lightly whipped and sweetened heavy cream

½ cup hot chocolate

1½ ounces Reposado tequila

½ ounce Frangelico

Spiced Sugar for garnish (PAGE 116)

Dried orange peel for garnish
(optional, see PAGE 75)

——— MAKES 1 DRINK ———

Gently stir together the orange brandy and whipped cream in a small bowl to combine. (The cream should be thickened, but still thin enough to pour.)

Combine the hot chocolate, tequila, and Frangelico in a mug or an Irish-coffee glass. Layer the orange cream on the drink by slowly pouring it over the back of a bar spoon. Sprinkle with the spiced sugar, and lay the strips of dried orange peel, if using, on the cream.

HOT TODDY

4 to 5 whole cloves

1 cinnamon stick

1 star anise

1 teaspoon honey

½ cup boiling water

1½ ounces brandy

Lemon wedge

——— MAKES 1 DRINK ———

Combine the cloves, cinnamon stick, star anise, and honey in a heat-proof snifter. Top with the boiling water and stir to melt the honey. Top with brandy. Squeeze the lemon wedge and drop into the snifter.

THE CURE

SHORT OF NOT DRINKING AT ALL, THE BEST WAY TO AVOID a hangover is to drink in moderation. Remember, cocktails are best sipped and enjoyed, not guzzled and gulped until you're so drunk that you can't see straight. Drinking moderately, and alternating between water and your cocktail, will help ensure that you don't wake up with jackhammers pounding in your head.

If you overdo it, you've got no choice but to suffer through the ever-dreaded hangover. Maybe you stayed up until the small hours of the morning mixing those last few cocktails, or maybe you just didn't eat enough or drink enough water. Regardless of what got you, there's nothing you can do about it now. Or is there? We're frequently asked for our favorite cure. Our answer is simple: water and time. Your body needs water to rehydrate, and time to recover. True, this isn't as interesting as sucking back a raw egg that has been doused with Worcestershire sauce, salt and pepper, and Tabasco sauce (a concoction otherwise known as a prairie oyster), but it is the only real cure we know for a hangover.

There are plenty of remedies out there that just might work for you. In the name of scientific research, we've taken an informal survey of a selection of our bartending and drinking friends and asked them for their favorite hangover cures. There were several common themes, such as reaching for a bit of the hair of the dog, sleeping until the day is gone, and taking a long, hot shower, to name a few. We've condensed our notes into a manageable list and, whenever appropriate, we've supplied recipes and our own thoughts about a particular "cure." Remember, our best recommendation for avoiding a hangover is moderation.

Hair of the Dog

Oddly enough, this was one of the most common recommendations we came across in our survey. Even though it served as the root of your morning pain, sipping on something boozy is commonly thought of as the perfect hangover cure. Folks at the restaurant frequently ask for a strong, spicy Bloody Mary. But a glass of Champagne, a **DEATH IN THE AFTERNOON** (Champagne with a splash of absinthe or Pernod), or even a plain old Screwdriver may do the trick just as well. If you're feeling particularly masochistic, you might want to try an Ernest Hemingway specialty known as Death in the Gulf Stream. This is a mixture of crushed ice, 4 dashes of Angostura bitters, the juice and peels of a whole lime, and an oversized shot of extra-dry Holland

BLOODY MARY

2 ounces vodka

¼ ounce lemon juice

¼ teaspoon Dijon mustard
(or to taste)

¼ teaspoon prepared horseradish
(or to taste)

2 to 3 dashes Worcestershire sauce
(or to taste)

2 to 3 dashes Tabasco
(or to taste)

2 pinches celery salt

1 pinch freshly grated black pepper

4 ounces Tomato Juice

Sweet pepper or olive, cocktail onion,
and lemon wedge, for garnish

——— MAKES 1 DRINK ———

Combine ingredients in an ice-filled pilsner glass. Top glass with a metal mixing tin and gently roll the cocktail over a few times to combine ingredients. Garnish with a sweet pepper or an olive, cocktail onion, and lemon wedge.

gin. As he said of the drink, "It is reviving and refreshing; it cools the blood and inspires renewed interest in food, companions and life" (quoted in Colin Peter Field's *The Cocktails of the Ritz Paris*, 2003).

Sleep

It's Saturday morning and your internal alarm clock has awakened you at nine, but your head is cursing you from the night before. What can you do? Get up, pour yourself a tall glass of cool water, and sip it down, then climb right back into bed and go to sleep again. We know some people who do get up, go out for a quick bite and a **BLOODY MARY,** and then return home to go back to sleep. The food-induced coma paired with the booze in the Bloody Mary helps them to fall asleep again. By the time they wake up a second time, they're feeling rested and revived.

Greasy Eats

There's something about greasy food that helps your body feel better after a night of serious drinking. It could be a supersized burrito, a big bowl of Mexican *menudo* with jalapeños and a cow's ankle, a burger and onion rings dripping with oil, or a big bowl of chow mein. Everyone has a different favorite, but a gut full of greasy food sure can help to soak up all the booze from the night before.

Hay Ride

This is a favorite cure that came up more often than we expected. Taking a roll in the sack with your favorite partner is a great way to forget the pains of a hangover. Maybe it's the exercise, like going surfing or taking a therapeutic bike ride, but we think it's something else entirely. One of our respondents summed it up best: "A couple of rum and Cokes and sex with a hottie. You'll still be hung over, but you just won't care!"

Hydration

Alcohol dehydrates your body, and when you wake up with a pounding headache in the morning, it is really your brain's way of saying that it is thirsty. Sip water before going to bed to start the rehydration process; it's the first step toward curing the impending morning hangover. Continue drinking water throughout the day, and your body will thank you. Sports drinks, complete with replenishing electrolytes, are another effective source of hydration. In fact, in our surveys more people recommended sipping on a favorite sports drink, instead of plain water, when trying to recover from a hangover.

DEATH
IN THE
AFTERNOON

¼ ounce pastis, preferably Pernod

Champagne

———————— MAKES 1 DRINK ————————

Pour the Pernod into a champagne
flute and fill with Champagne.

SUGGESTED READING

WE'VE MANAGED TO SPEND COUNTLESS HOURS, NOT TO MENTION DOLLARS, on the Internet, in used bookstores, at swap meets, and at yard sales in order to build up our modest collections of classic-cocktail books, some of which are out of print. There are plenty of excellent cocktail and spirits books on the market. Some, like Jerry Thomas's *How To Mix Drinks,* are old volumes that have recently been reissued. Others, like Ted Haigh's *Vintage Spirits and Forgotten Cocktails,* are new books that celebrate lost classics and obscure drinks. Below are some of our favorites. You will probably find other books that tickle your fancy. Happy hunting!

Adams, Jad. *Hideous Absinthe: A History of the Devil in a Bottle*. Madison, Wisc.: University of Wisconsin Press, 2004.

Baker, Charles H., Jr. *Jigger, Beaker, & Glass: Drinking Around the World*. 1946. Reprint, Lanham, Md.: The Derrydale Press, 1992.

Baker, Phil. *The Book of Absinthe: A Cultural History*. New York: Grove Press, 2001.

Beebe, Lucius. *The Stork Club Bar Book*. 1946. Reprint. Winston-Salem, North Carolina: New Day Publishing, 2003.

Blue, Anthony Dias. *The Complete Book of Spirits: A Guide to Their History, Production, and Enjoyment*. New York: HarperCollins, 2004.

Bullock, Tom, and D.J. Frienz. *173 Pre-Prohibition Cocktails: Potations So Good They Scandalized a President*. Jenks, Okla.: Howling at the Moon Press, 2001.

Conrad, Barnaby, III. *Absinthe: History in a Bottle*. San Francisco: Chronicle Books, 1988.

____. *The Martini: An Illustrated History of an American Classic*. San Francisco: Chronicle Books, 1995.

Craddock, Harry. *The Savoy Cocktail Book*. 1930. Reprint, London: Pavilion Books Limited, 1999.

Crocket, Albert Stevens. *The Old Waldorf Astoria Bar Book*. 1935. Reprint, The J. Peterman Company, 1998.

Degroff, Dale. *The Craft of The Cocktail*. New York: Clarkson Potter, 2002.

Edmonds, Lowell. *Martini, Straight Up: The Classic American Cocktail*. Baltimore: Johns Hopkins University Press, 1998.

Field, Colin Peter. *The Cocktails of The Ritz Paris*. New York: Simon & Schuster, 2003.

Grimes, William. *Straight Up or on the Rocks: The Story of the American Cocktail*. New York: North Point Press, 2001.

Haigh, Ted. *Vintage Spirits & Forgotten Cocktails: From the Alamagoozlum Cocktail to the Zombie, 80 Rediscovered Recipes and the Stories Behind Them*. Gloucester, Mass.: Quarry Books, 2004.

Harrington, Paul. *Cocktail: The Drinks Bible For The 21st Century*. New York: Viking Penguin, 1998.

Herbst, Sharon Tyler, and Ron Herbst. *The Ultimate A-To-Z Bar Guide*. New York: Broadway Books, 1998.

Jackson, Michael. *Michael Jackson's Bar & Cocktail Companion: The Connoisseur's Handbook*. Philadelphia, Penn.: Running Press, 1994.

Regan, Gary, and Mardee Haidin Regan. *New Classic Cocktails*. New York: Wiley Publishing, 1997.

Regan, Gary. *The Joy of Mixology: The Consummate Guide to the Bartender's Craft*. New York: Clarkson Potter, 2003.

Thomas, Jerry. *How To Mix Drinks, or The Bon-Vivant's Companion*. 1862. Reprint. Winston-Salem, North Carolina: New Day Publishing, 2004.

Wondrich, David. *Esquire Drinks: An Opinionated & Irreverent Guide to Drinking*. New York: Hearst Books, 2002.

____. *Killer Cocktails: An Intoxicating Guide to Sophisticated Drinking*. New York: HarperCollins, 2005.

INDEX

TABLE OF EQUIVALENTS

Liquid Measurements

1 bar spoon	½ ounce
1 teaspoon	⅙ ounce
1 tablespoon	½ ounce
2 tablespoons (1 pony)	1 ounce
3 tablespoons (1 jigger)	1½ ounces

¼ cup	2 ounces
⅓ cup	2.6 ounces
½ cup	4 ounces
⅔ cup	5.2 ounces
¾ cup	6 ounces
1 cup	8 ounces
1 pint	16 ounces
1 quart	32 ounces

750 ml bottle	25.4 ounces
1 liter bottle	33.8 ounces